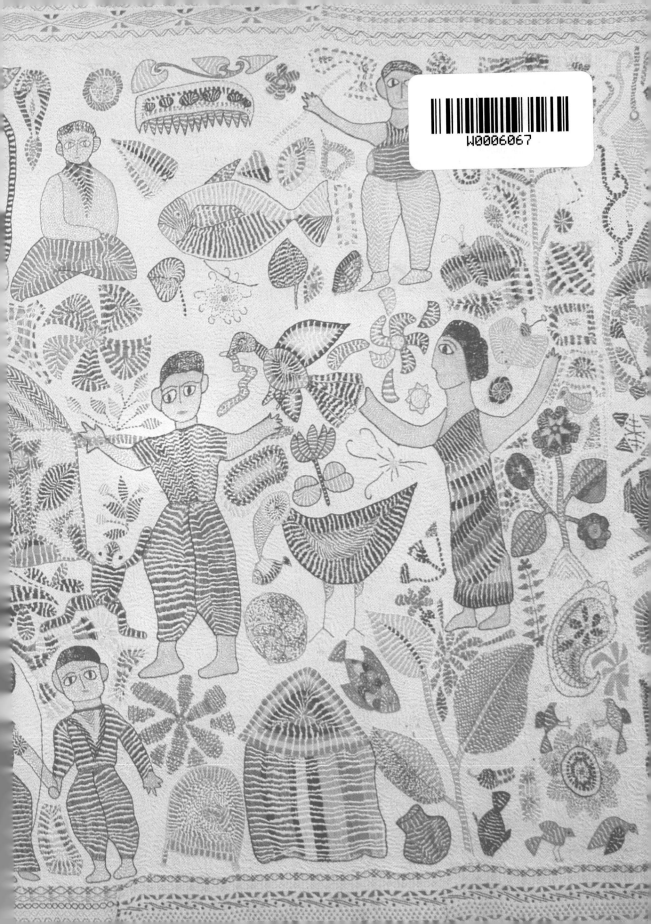

THE ART OF KANTHA EMBROIDERY

Niaz Zaman

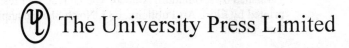

The University Press Limited

The University Press Limited
Red Crescent Building
114 Motijheel Commercial Area
G P O Box 2611
Dhaka 1000
Bangladesh

Fax: (88 02) 9565443
E-mail: upl@bttb.net
Website: www.uplbooks.com

Second Revised Edition 1993
First published 1981
Reprinted 2000

Book design and cover by
Tofazzal Hossain

Photographs by
Mustafizur Rahman, Saadot Hossain, Salahuddin Azizee,
Shamsuzzaman, M. A. Sadek, Swapan Saha, Adcom.

Drawings by
Kajal

ISBN 984 05 1228 5

Published by Mohiuddin Ahmed, The University Press Limited, and
printed by Elora Art Publicity, 635, North Shahjahanpur, Dhaka,
Bangladesh.

To
The women of Bangladesh
without whom this book
would never have been

Contents

Map   vi

Preface   vii

Introduction   1

The Kantha Tradition   8

Old Threads for New   22

Making a Kantha   27

The Influence of Religion and Folk Belief   36

Kantha Stitches   44

Different Kantha Articles   60

Kantha Motifs   64

Kantha Borders   94

Different Types of Kanthas   108

Regional Differences in Kanthas   124

Kantha Revival   139

Kantha Collections   159

Bibliography   161

Glossary   165

Index   171

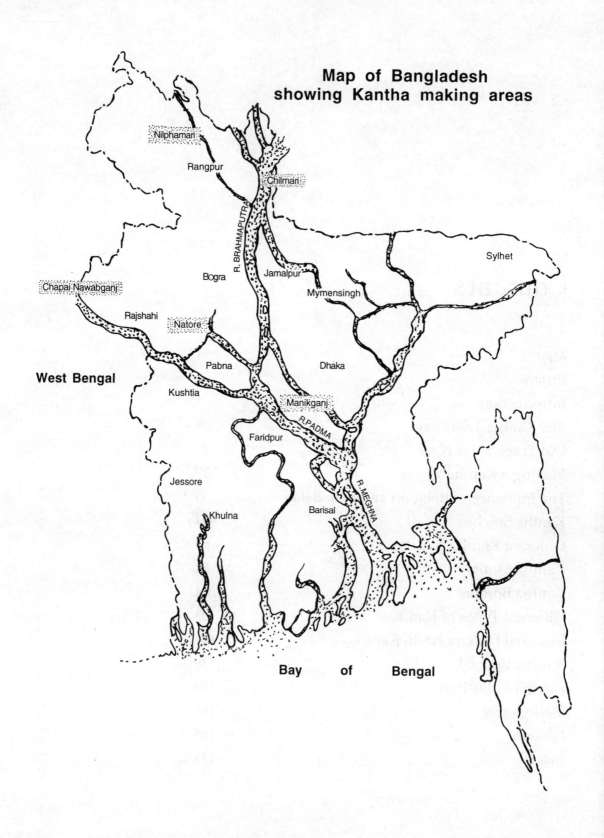

**Map of Bangladesh
showing Kantha making areas**

Nilphamari

Rangpur

Chilmari

R. BRAHMAPUTRA

Sylhet

Bogra

Jamalpur

Mymensingh

Chapai Nawabganj

Rajshahi

Natore

Dhaka

Pabna

West Bengal

Kushtia

Manikganj

R.PADMA

Faridpur

R. MEGHNA

Jessore

Khulna

Barisal

Bay   of   Bengal

Preface

In 1976, a chance remark by my sister-in-law, Mrs. Zebunnessa Majid, aroused my interest in kanthas. While I had been fascinated by Jasimuddin's poem, *Nakshi Kanthar Maath*, or as E. M. Milford translates it, *The Field of the Embroidered Quilt*, I had not seen an embroidered quilt of the type Jasimuddin had described. True, I has seen kanthas made of red *salu*, embroidered in large cross stitch, and, because I was fortunate to have a friend who came from Rajshahi, had also seen *lohori* kanthas. However, in order to see the type of kantha that had inspired Jasimuddin, I had to go to the Dhaka Museum, still located at Nimtali at the time, and request the Curator, Dr. Enamul Haque, to let me see the kanthas locked in boxes for want of space.

Today one does not have to try as hard to see kanthas—though, unfortunately, the finest pieces are still locked in boxes. Handicraft shops offer kanthas for sale, television programmes utilize kanthas as backdrops or counterpanes in bedroom scenes, ministerial offices, conference rooms, hotel lobbies use kanthas to give an authentic Bangladeshi touch. Emerging from the private, inner recesses of homes and locked boxes, kanthas have invaded public space. To what do we owe this resurgence? A number of factors were perhaps responsible: a sense of national identity and the emergence worldwide of interest in ethnic art. The catalyst, however, seemed to be the commissioning of large pieces for a new five-star hotel in the mid-eighties.

It was shortly after the first edition of this book that the kantha revival took place. In this short space of time, however, the kantha has also changed, producing hybrid forms which kantha *aficionados* would not refer to as kantha. However, these forms have been influenced by the kantha and are, in turn, influencing kanthas. It is therefore interesting that whereas in the first edition I spoke of kanthas as belonging to the past, in this edition, even as I talk of kantha being a living art form, I must talk of changes that are setting in and, as some might even think, are destroying the kantha. Furthermore, an associate of a handicrafts outlet seems to think that a saturation point has been reached as far as kanthas are concerned. "Everyone in Bangladesh who is interested in kanthas already has a couple. What do the 5000 women trained in kantha making do?" Similarly kantha makers at another organization mourned that there were no more demands for large kanthas and therefore no work for them. However, such prognostications are unnecessarily gloomy. Kanthas have become integrated into our cultural life. Though the demand may lessen, though shoddy pieces as well as hybrid forms may continue to flood the handicrafts market, a few exquisite pieces will be produced, pieces that might well rival museum acquisitions.

This revised edition includes almost all the material that was included in the first, but there are additions necessitated by the kantha revival. The last chapter is entirely new, but almost each chapter has had some alterations made because of the changes that have taken place in the kantha. I also attempt to document, before all differences are wiped out, the regional differences in kanthas.

For this edition there are a number of people whom I must thank, people without whom this book would not have been possible. There is first of all Lala Rukh who invited me to speak at an ECOTA workshop, and thereby reawakened an interest that absence from the country had made dormant—particularly as so much had happened to the kantha in the years I had been away. I would also like to thank Sayyada R. Ghuznavi, Hameeda Hossain and Razia Qadir for filling me in on all that took place during the years I was out of the country. To Mr. Tofail Ahmed and Mohammad Sayeedur I owe a debt of gratitude for sharing their knowledge of what has been, for both of them, a life-long vocation. I would like to record my gratitude to Surayia Rahman for discussing her work. I also thank the workers at Kumudini, BRAC, and Skill Development for Underprivileged Women for their patience in answering questions. For permission to photograph kanthas in their collection I would like to thank the National Museum, Mrs. Jahanara Abedin, Kumudini, SDUW, the Bangla Academy, Mr. Tofail Ahmed, Dr. Parveen Rashid, Professor Zahurul Huque, Mrs. Rokeya Kabir. Kantha photographs were also provided by Adcom and Swapan Saha.

I wish also to express my gratitude to my long-suffering family, particularly my husband, Qazi Siddiquzzaman, who carefully guarded my notes and files all the years I was away from the country. It is true he managed to lose my desk, but he was careful to preserve all the scraps of paper in it. How necessary these were only I know.

I owe a very special debt of gratitude to Mrs. Joya Pati of Kumudini for supporting this revision in various ways. It was her suggestion of a second edition that encouraged me to consider an updated version. Without her support this revision would perhaps not have materialized. I thank her once again.

October 25, 1993   NIAZ ZAMAN

Introduction

In 1981 a new five-star hotel was opened in Dhaka, the capital of Bangladesh. The name chosen for the hotel was Sonargaon—the Golden Village—a name which harkened back to the golden past of Bengal when the granaries were full of paddy and the ponds full of fish. The days of golden Bengal were long over—if they ever existed, except in legend and lore. Floods, famine, food shortage, dependence on external aid had become the rule rather than the exception long before the hotel was planned. But in its plan and conception, the hotel symbolized and embodied the best that Golden Bengal could offer. It was, therefore, only in order, that the decoration pieces that were to furnish the hotel should be truly indigenous. And what could be more representative than the kantha, or the embroidered quilt of Bengal? Therefore, when the hotel opened, across its lobby wall and in the foyer were proudly displayed specially commissioned kanthas. Newly made, they yet represented an old tradition, a tradition that had almost been forgotten, and was made new again by this proud display.

It is true that kanthas and kantha making were never dead. Every poor woman in the villages and towns of Bangladesh continued to stitch kanthas as women had in the past—putting together old saris and *lungis* when their initial purpose had been served and the cloth become too frail and worn out through repeated washings to stand up to further wear. Outside the dismal huts in every slum, cotton quilts hung up to air and dry. In most middle-class families as well, kanthas were used instead of light

Shostir chinho

blankets during cool nights. But these were put together with a minimum of needlework and were meant for private use, not public display. The kind of kantha that the Sonargaon hotel displayed was a thing of the past. Different modes of life and different ideas of aesthetics had caused a fading of interest in indigenous art. The two-hundred-year domination of the Indian subcontinent by the British had led to a substitution of the western for the indigenous, whether it was in language, dress, education, or art.

In the early years of the twentieth century, the struggle for independence and the *swadeshi* movement led to the evocation of an Indian identity. Deep-seated emotions, however, soon led, as is well-known, to the two-nation theory and the sense of a Pakistani identity, separate from an Indian one. The attempt at creating a Pakistani identity, however, broke down soon after partition. The proclamation that Urdu alone would be the state language of Pakistan led to protests in East Pakistan as early as 1948. In 1952, the language struggle reached such an extreme that people in Dhaka city broke Section 144—prohibiting the gathering of more than three persons—to demand that Bangla be recognized as one of the state languages of Pakistan. Over the years, the celebrations during February, commemorating the Language Movement and the Language martyrs, had emerged in a distinctly Bengali culture. Centering upon the Language Movement grew a Bangladeshi cultural awareness that consciously opposed the cultural domination of Pakistan. This awareness led to the adoption of an indigenous art form at comme-morations of the language struggle. The women's art of *alpana* in particular was used to ornament the paths around the Shaheed Minar, the monument marking the spot where young Bengalis had laid down their lives.

While *alpana* art was used almost defiantly in the face of the Pakistani masters who could not appreciate the art of the *alpana*, and also hated and feared it as unIslamic and suggestive of black magic, the art of the kantha was an almost forgotten one. Kanthas had disappeared from public view, so that when people spoke of the *nakshi* kantha, Jasimudin's poem *Nakshi Kanthar Maath* was usually understood. In 1954, Tofail Ahmed mourned the kantha as a lost art, fated to be remembered because a folk poet had immortalized it in a poem, rather than as an article of common use. During Pakistan times, Zainul Abedin and Qamrul Hasan attempted to give a rightful place to indigenous art. Qamrul Hasan's attempt materialized in the shape of the Design Centre. But apathy and neglect allowed the traditional arts of Bangladesh to languish, and, in place of the traditional kanthas, a hybrid product, locally known as the "carpet" kantha, was made at the East Pakistan Small and Cottage Industries Corporation project at Chapai Nawabganj. Zainul Abedin, apart from setting up the Art College—now the Institute of Fine Arts—also advocated the setting up of a folk art museum and personally collected fine specimens of Jessore kanthas. It was only after liberation, however, that Zainul Abedin's dream of a folk arts museum materialized in the shape of the Folk Art and Crafts Foundation at Sonargaon.

During pre-liberation days, women's associations that encouraged women to develop skills that they could put to marketable use settled for traditional skills such as neddlework but not to the special type of needlework that is kantha embroidery. The revival of the kantha could only take place after the sense of national identity created a demand for the truly indigenous to replace the exogenous culture that was being discarded. In addition, economic necessity encouraged the development of traditional skills. It was, therefore, a number of factors that encouraged the revival of the kantha, even if somewhat hesitantly and tentatively, after the emergence of Bangladesh. In "Organising Women's Employment Through Kantha Production," Hameeda Hossain describes how kantha making was set up soon after Bangladesh became independent. The War of Independence in 1971 had left many women widowed or separated from their families. Attempts to rehabilitate them led, particularly in districts with a strong kantha tradition such as Jessore, Kushtia, Faridpur and Rajshahi, to setting up cottage industries and attempting to market kanthas as commercial products.

This attempt to revive kanthas was, however, not immediately successful. The kantha revival took a back seat to the development of jute handicrafts and then, a little later, to the jamdani revival. It was not surprising that one of the first handicrafts to be developed after liberation should have been jute, for example, floor coverings, place mats, and the *shika*—or pot hanger. After all, one of the sore points of the East Pakistani had been that the foreign exchange received through sale of jute, had gone to enrich West Pakistan. The initial flurry over jute, however, gradually faded. On the other hand, interest in the kantha, begun on a low key in early 1972—it was, after all, a domestic art, something that belonged to the private, not public sphere—gradually gained momentum. The display in Hotel Sonargaon and exhibitions held in the early eighties revealed the possibilities of the kantha as art form as well as income-generating activity.

The exhibitions and the attractive products at numerous handicraft stores have succeeded in attracting considerable interest both from foreign visitors as well as from Bangladeshis themselves, who are realizing for the first time—as a group—how beautiful kanthas can be. While these kanthas reflect a growing interest in the truly indigenous or ethnic art of Bangladesh, they also reflect the changes in this traditional art. Made of new cloth, made to order, embroidered by several women who have been given strict instructions about thread, colours, stitches, who have been given cloth with motifs and designs traced ready for them to begin sewing, these pieces of tapestry are still within the kantha tradition. Designs and motifs are drawn from old kanthas.

As the revival of the kantha has been closely linked with the revival of handicrafts, a brief summary of the role played by different organizations is useful. In pre-liberation Bangladesh, East Pakistan Small and Cottage Industries Corporation—now Bangladesh Small and Cottage Industries Corporation—had, for several years, run a project in Chapai Nawabganj. This project, however, produced only a hybrid form of kantha locally known as "carpet" kantha. These kanthas were worked with large cross stitches, a non-indigenous stitch. The motifs, however, were indigenous ones, ranging from various floral motifs to local fauna—deer, peacocks, elephants. The cloth, a deep red cloth, locally known as *lal salu*, was the same used for *sujnis*, embroidered quilts popular in the Rajshahi area, but using small back stitches to embroider arabesque designs.

After 1972, the kantha revival was helped by numerous other organizations which emerged. The first of these organizations was the Bangladesh Handicraft Cooperative Federation with its outlet Karika. Closely associated with BSCIC, BHCF was, however, also more enterprising and innovative than BSCIC which, like most government enterprises, suffered from various forms of inertia. Hameeda Hossain, Perveen Ahmed, Ruby Ghuznavi, Lila Amirul Islam, who were closely associated with Karika in its initial stages, pulled out the kantha, so to speak, from the closed trunks in which it had long lain and displayed it at the outlet. Karika was followed by Aarong—the outlet for the Mennonite Church Council and then for Bangladesh Rural Advancement Committee—and Kumudini. In 1985 these organizations were followed by Skill Development for Underprivileged Women—or Nakshi Kantha Kendra—and then Arshi. SDUW and Arshi, unlike the other organizations, are wholly devoted to embroidery, which, though not strictly kantha embroidery, has been influenced by it. These organizations have been joined recently by Aranya.

Because the revival of the kantha has been closely associated with these organizations, certain changes in the tradition of the kantha have been unavoidable. While each of these organizations aims at developing traditional crafts, they are also commercial organizations. The development of a traditional craft is therefore also closely linked with the market. Will it sell ? And how much are people willing to pay for it?

As a result of these factors, a tremendous change is taking place in the kantha. Apart from new uses being found for the kantha, there are also changes in design, material and stitching. It is true that the kantha, even originally, served a number of functions. Thus it could be a large-sized wrapper, but it was also used as an *ashon* or seating place, a *gilaf* or quran cover, *bostani* or wrapper for precious garments, an *arshilata* or covering for combs and mirrors, a *balisher oshar* or pillow cover, and a *dastarkhan* or long placemat to be spread on the floor for dining. However, additional uses are being found for kanthas. Thus kanthas are being used as wall-hangings. And kantha embroidery is finding its way into cushion covers, ornamental yokes or panels for dresses, *kurtas*, saris, and purses.

Wall-hangings, ranging in size from several feet long to a few inches square, have perhaps effected the greatest change in kanthas. Originally kanthas were meant to be spread. Hence most kanthas had a central lotus which acted as the focal point of the kantha. The four corner motifs—*kalkas* or paisleys and *brikshalatas* or tree-of life motifs—all verged on this central motif. Furthermore, the background stitching tended to swirl around each motif, almost moulding the motifs in the process. Today, because kanthas are meant to be hung and viewed frontally, both the design and the stitching have undergone a change. Thus, instead of a centre and four corners, many kanthas have a top and a bottom. Furthermore, as the kantha is designed by a designer and the designs then traced onto the kantha which is given to craftswomen to embroider, the needle is not used to mark out the motifs to be filled. The naive, transparent figures of traditional kanthas were the result of the needlewoman using her needle to embroider the motifs, both the *mahout* and the elephant, for instance. Nowadays this transparent effect is occasionally deliberately created in the interest of tradition. Furthermore, with all the designs being traced onto the cloth, the needlewoman no longer needs to swirl around motifs but fills in the gaps between them. The moulding effect is, therefore, often missing from these kanthas.

One of the most striking differences in background stitching may be seen in the "kanthas" of Skill Development for Underprivileged Women. Catering to a sophisticated taste, the SDUW "kanthas" have eliminated the ripple effect of traditional kanthas in their wall-hangings. The characteristic kantha stitch is a ripple stitch. The SDUW "kanthas," however, use the darning stitch, thus creating a smooth surface instead of the rippled one created by the kantha stitch. Furthermore, the "kanthas" at SDUW are embroidered on silk, rather than on cotton. A wide gulf therefore separates them from the traditional kanthas embroidered on old cloth with thread drawn from sari borders. Aarong and Kumudini, on the other hand, have attempted to remain closer to traditional kanthas in form and spirit, though even they have been forced to change to cater to the demands of the market, both local and foreign.

It is perhaps a sad truth that our rich tradition could only be revived when a market value was put on it. At the same time it should be borne in mind that the revival of the kantha has benefited thousands of women who would otherwise not have been gainfully employed—BRAC, for instance, utilizes the work of 3000 women at Jamalpur and 2000 women at Jessore; Kumudini estimates that it has trained over 8000 women since the kantha project began. While it is true that our traditional craft is no longer in the hands of the maker, but in that of organizations who know what will sell and what will not, it should be remembered that these organizations have the resources and the initiative to turn back to a past when the tradition was alive and well. If the kanthas that these organizations make are well beyond the reach of the common man or woman, it is perhaps to their credit that they have elevated what was valueless, except sentimentally, into invaluable art.

The Kantha Tradition

Quilting is not unique to Bangladesh. In some form or other it is practised in almost all lands where winters are cool or cold. However, the form that quilting has taken in Bengal is unique, with the indigenous quilt or kantha (pronounced variously kāṅthā, kaeṅthā, kethā, khetā) reflecting the blend of several factors that form the cultural identity of this land. Apart from being a functional article, the kantha is also an example of folk art, particularly women's art.

Folk art emerges from a combination of material circumstances and daily needs. Climate, geography and economic factors play their role. Religious beliefs and superstitions guide choice of motifs. These factors are also true of the kantha. Though the winters of Bangladesh are fairly mild, there is a need for some sort of covering. The kantha developed mainly out of this need for a covering for our mild winters as well as our cool monsoon nights. The long rainy days gave the women of Bengal the much needed leisure to stitch together the several layers of cloth that make up the kantha. Folk art has always been composed of material most readily available. The area comprising Bangladesh was, from earliest times, a cotton growing and weaving area. Thus the material used was cotton textile, traditionally, old saris, *lungis* or *dhotis* that had been through many washes and become too frail for wear.

Waste has not been part of traditional cultures, and the women of Bengal carefully put away worn-out saris,

Nineteenth-century kantha from Faridpur

Kantha from Jessore depicting the goddess Lakshmi

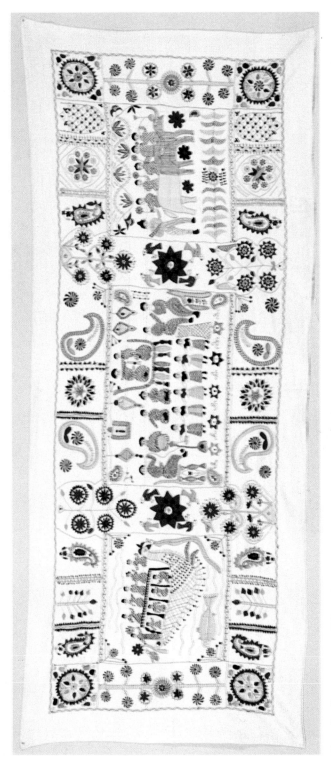

Popular Sonargaon wall-hanging

A Tale of Two Villages: Wall-hanging designed by Surayia Rahman
based on *Nakshi Kanthar Maath*

dhotis and *lungis* until enough material had been collected to, make a kantha. Then, layering those old pieces of worn-out cloth, the women of Bengal stitched them together with loving care to produce coverlets and wraps. But they also made other objects of functional or devotional use. Putting together smaller scraps of material they made *ashons* for seating honoured guests or for performing *puja* ; they made *dastarkhans* to spread on the floor for a dining cloth; they made *arshilatas* to cover mirrors and combs; they made *balisher oshars* to cover pillows to prevent perspiration and hair oil soaking the pillow. But the women of Bengal did not just utilize worn-out material to make articles of daily use; they also used intricate variations of the simple running stitch to embellish those articles with motifs drawn from their rich cultural life to create fine works of art. As Kamaladevi Chattopadhaya comments, "Kantha is an example of a strange contradiction, for here is an object created at an endeavor at thrift by transforming wornout textile that would normally be thrown away, into objects of rare beauty and which have in course of time become legendary."[1]

We do not know when the simple stitches that hold the several layers together turned into the exquisite needlework that marks the kantha. What we *do* know is that the art of embroidery in India is very old. There are references to needles as far back as the *Rgveda*, and garments worn were often embroidered.[2] Megasthenes, writing about the court of Chandragupta, noted that the nobles wore dresses worked in gold adorned with precious stones and also flowered robes of fine muslin.

Western writers too mention the embroidery of India. Writing in 1888, George Birdwood praised the quality of Indian embroidery. So excellent was the work that the Portuguese sent satin to be embroidered by Indians according to European designs—and caused the

---

1. *Indian Embroidery* (New Delhi, 1975), p. 55.
2. Abinas Chandra Das, *Rgvedic Culture* (Calcutta, 1925), p. 212.

infiltration of European designs into India. Describing the embroidery of Bengal, Birdwood referred to Dhaka *chikan* and Dhaka *kashida*, which were in demand throughout India, Persia, Europe, Egypt, and Turkey. Birdwood was, however, talking about embroidery on new cloth, not embroidery on old cloth.

References to kanthas appear in Bengali folk lore and fairy tale handed down through generations. Mohammad Sayeedur Rahman, for example, describes how the 12th century legendary Raja Gopichandra accepted a kantha and a *jhola* or bag on becoming an ascetic.

> Napit aniya Raja mastak moraila.
> Golay kheta diya mukhe bhusan charaila.
> Baglay bagli dila singhanad golay.
> Chakmaki pather dila batua adhari.
> Ghor meghli dila rasher khapri.[1]

> The barber came and shaved the Raja's head.
> Wrapping the Raja's neck with a kantha
> He adorned his throat with jewels.
> Placing a bag in his arms,
> He put a purse with a flintstone in his hand.
> On the Raja's forehead he placed a red sandalwood spot
> And round his waist he wrapped a dark sarong.

Mohammad Sayeedur Rahman points out that Muslim saints, such as Ghazi *pir*, Monai *pir*, Khizr *pir*, Bhola *pir*, Chindi *pir* also used old cloth and patchwork. In Baul songs as well, the tradition of the kantha finds a place in metaphor and simile.

> Aasmaan jora fakirre bhai.
> Jamin jora ketha
> Eshob fakir morlay paray
> Er kabar hobey kotha rey.[2]

> The friend of the fakirs is the sky.
> The friend of the earth is the kantha.
> When these fakirs die
> Where will their graves lie?

---

1. Quoted in Mohammad Sayeedur Rahman, "The Common Ground" in *Woven Air* (London, 1988), p. 23.
2. Rahman, "The Common Ground," p. 24.

The kantha often figures in fairy stories as a humble article of daily use or as a magical object with fabulous properties. Thus, in the tale of the foolish brother and the clever brother, a kantha is one of the objects that the brothers have in common. While the clever brother has the use of the kantha at night—and therefore can use it to the full-the foolish brother has the use of it during the daytime—and therefore must sun it and occasionally wash it without ever enjoying its warmth. It is only after a wise old man gives the foolish brother some good advice that both brothers share it equally. There is also a variant of this story, with the brothers being replaced by two old women. In the fairy story of *Buddhu Bhutum* as well a kantha figures prominently. In this story a Monkey Prince and an Owl Prince, named Buddhu and Bhutum respectively, the youngest sons of a king by his sixth and seventh queens, go in search of a princess. They find her at the bottom of the sea. Like all princesses, she has several tricks to escape marriage, but Buddhu is a clever prince and manages to overcome all difficulties. In the process he also manages to get a kantha with the magical properties of raising an army of soldiers. Needless to say, this army of soldiers helps the two princes get back their rightful share of the throne.[1]

In literature also there are references to the kantha; for example, Nazrul Islam uses the image of a kantha to describe a winter morning. The land snuggles under a winter mist much as a man snuggles under a kantha.

> Usha didir uthar agge uthbo pahar chure
> Dekhbo niche ghumay shahar shiter kantha mure.[2]

> I shall awake before the dawn does,
> And from the mountain top
> I shall look down and see the town asleep
> Wrapped in a winter kantha.

---

1. The stories of the old women and the monkey prince are available as "The Story of the Half Chicken" and "Princess Kalabati and the Monkey Prince" in my translation *Animal Tales from Bangladesh*.

2. "Ghum Jagano Pakhi," *Shrestha Kabita* (Dhaka, 1974), p. 14.

All these references to the kantha are, however, to the humble quilt. In fact, the kantha, as in the case of Raja Gopichandra, was associated with penury. There is thus the well-known Bengali proverb, "Chhira kanthaye shuye, rajprasader shapna dehka." That is, one may sleep on a ragged kantha and dream of a king's palace. In other words, a poor man who possesses a kantha can very well dream of being rich but riches are beyond his grasp. These early references to the kantha do not mention the exquisite embroidery that marks the best kanthas.

Writing in the early 1920's, Girish Chandra Vedantatirtha noted how kanthas were used mainly by poor people, not by the rich:" Samriddha bilashir sahit ihar samparka dekha jaye na."[1]

Perhaps the first person to recognize the significance of the kantha and its association with the lives of the women of rural Bengal was Jasimuddin, the poet of the Bengal countryside. In his *Nakshi Kanthar Maath,* or The Field of the Embroidered Quilt, he immortalized the kantha, and succeeded so well that the appellation *nakshi* prefaces the word "kantha" whenever we wish to talk about the quilt. This is particularly when we wish to distinguish it from the humble quilt from which all embroidered quilts originated. Before the kantha revival of the early eighties, Jasimuddin's poem had become better known than the article itself. In fact, when the average Bengali spoke of the *nakshi* kantha or heard the term, it was the poem that was referred to or understood, not the quilt so lovingly and painstakingly put together by the women of Bengal. As Tofail Ahmed noted in 1964, with the change in taste and life-styles, the kantha was becoming a lost art. He suggested that it would be in Jasimuddin's poem alone that the kantha would be preserved. "Drishtibhangi o paribartaner sange purba Pakistaner e gana shilpa lupta hoye jacche. Pallikabi Jasimuddiner 'Nakshi Kanthar Maather' bhitar diye amar thakbe e lupta shilper smriti."[2]

1. *Prachin Shilpa Parichay* (Introduction to Ancient Arts and Crafts) (Calcutta: 1972), p.32.
2. *Amader Prachin Shilpa* (Dhaka , 1964), p. 54.

Twenty years later, with kanthas displayed proudly in lobbies and drawing rooms, Tofail Ahmed's lament seems incongruous. Nevertheless, Jasimuddin has become, as Ahmed says, inextricably linked with the kantha. In fact, his use of the term "nakshi kantha" has resulted in a change in nomenclature. "Nakshi kantha" has become the name for the kantha in Bangladesh. It should be noted that most early writers on the kantha used the term "kantha" by itself. Thus Dinesh Chandra Sen, who was perhaps the first person to discuss the artistry of the kantha and devoted three pages to kanthas in *Brihat Banga* in 1935, did not use the term "nakshi kantha." Stella Kramrisch, the first westerner to discuss the kantha as an art form, was also content to refer to the quilt simply as "kantha." Gurusaday Dutt, an I.C.S. officer whose travels in Bengal helped him discover and collect specimens of this art—and later to build the famous collection that is the Gurusaday Collection—also used the term "kantha" in his essay, "The Art of Kantha," in the Calcutta *Modern Review*. So too does Ajit Mookerjee, who includes the kantha as an example of one of the folk arts of Bengal in his book, *The Folk Art of Bengal*.

Jasimuddin, as he tells us in an essay in *Mashik Mohammadi*, had collected kanthas for Dinesh Chandra Sen. Some of these kanthas were later used by Sen's colleague to illustrate *Brihat Banga*. Jasimuddin had also heard the painter Abindranath Tagore's account of a kantha seen in Sylhet. This kantha had been embroidered by a woman who had begun it as a young bride and had continued to embroider into the kantha all the subsequent incidents that took place in her life. Inspired by the kanthas he had seen, and even more by the kantha he had not seen, Jasimuddin wrote *Nakshi Kanthar Maath* in which the kantha becomes the symbol of Shaju's life as well as the reflection of the life of every Bengali village woman.

The poem tells the story of two young lovers who lived in two different villages. One village was crowded with huts but the other was sparsely populated, and only one or two huts peeped out from among the trees. Between the villages were broad fields of grain, and beside the fields there was a lovely lake on which floated the hundred-petalled lotuses. Rupa belonged to one village, Shaju to the other. Shaju was a lovely maiden. Her lips were red, her hair was black, and her skin the colour of golden marigolds. Girls were strictly guarded in the village, especially girls who had no father to protect them. But, despite all restrictions, Rupa and Shaju saw each other and fell in love. They finally got married, but they were not fated to live happily ever after. Rupa had to leave the village, and Shaju, during his absence, pined away and died. Rupa came back too late. All that was left of Shaju was the embroidered quilt which she had begun as an unmarried maiden and that she had continued all the days of her life, embroidering into it her joys and her sorrows. She had drawn herself as a happy bride, but she had also drawn her grave, knowing that without Rupa she might as well be dead.

In *Nakshi Kanthar Maath* Jasimuddin imaginatively recreated how a village maiden might embroider her kantha. Like other traditional Bengali maidens, Shaju embroiders into the kantha her hopes and fears, her joys and sorrows. She does not speak, but the pictures she draws with her needle tell us all she would.

> Spreading the embroidered quilt
> She works the livelong night,
> As if the quilt her poet were
> Of her bereaved plight.
> Many a joy and many a sorrow
> Is written on its breast;
> The story of Rupa's life is there,
> Line by line expressed.[1]

Jasimuddin describes how Shaju begins the kantha when she is young and happy. She continues to embroider it as she grows older.

1. *The Field of the Embroidered Quilt*, Tr. E. M. Milford. Rev. W. McDermott (Dhaka 1964).

She is a daughter beloved at home
When the embroidery begins,
Later a husband sits at her side,
Her red lips hum as she sings.

Shaju's happiness does not last very long. The husband she loves has to flee the village. Shaju sits down with the same quilt, but, instead of scenes of joy, she portrays the sorrowful scenes etched in her memory.

The self-same quilt she opens
But those days ne'er return.
Those golden dreams of joy have vanished,
To ashes grey they burn.

So, added to the picture of their wedding, added to the home of Rupa, she now adds the scene of farewell, draws her husband turning to say goodbye, draws her own dishevelled face.

Stitch by stitch she carefully draws
The last scene of pain,
The farewell of Rupa, slowly going,
Then turning a little again.
Turning again to the cottage home,
At the door his peasant wife
Standing dishevelled, gazing at him
Who is going to leave her for life.

Shaju imagines her own death and embroiders a tomb. What Shaju foresees takes place. Rupa returns to find Shaju dead. Shaju could not live without Rupa; Rupa too cannot live without Shaju. Wrapping himself in the quilt that he finds on her grave, he too dies.

Inspired by the quilts of Bengal, Jasimuddin's *Nakshi Kanthar Maath* recreated imaginatively how a Bengali woman might have told the story of her life in the only way open to her. Because Jasimuddin was a poet, he suggested the complete spontaneity and freedom with which a woman might embroider a kantha. Usually, however, what we see in the old kanthas that have been preserved in museums is a certain generic similarity. As Kamaladevi Chattopadhaya notes in *Handicrafts of India*, while the kantha has limitless designs because the women

who embroidered the kanthas could make any innovation
they fancied, usually there is a basic traditional design in
their work. At the centre of most kanthas, forming the
focal point of the design, is a lotus. In the four corners of
the kantha—or in the four corners of the square that
contains the lotus—are embroidered tree-of-life motifs that
point towards the lotus. In the available spaces are
embroidered motifs and symbols drawn from a common
stock. Similarly, scenes in kanthas were generally drawn
from myths and legends or from the familiar surroundings
of these adept needlewomen. Favourite scenes, for
example, were those of palanquins being borne by bearers,
or a marriage ceremony, the bride and groom seated side
by side. It was not the needlewoman's own marriage that
was thus depicted, but rather the marriage which formed
so essential a part of the culture of an agrarian society
dependent on the fertility of the soil.

That Jasimuddin's kantha, while based on the kanthas
he had seen or heard of, was a creation of his vivid
imagination is also clear from the fact that in Abindranath
Tagore's account it is not a young unmarried girl like
Shaju who begins the kantha but a young bride.
Furthermore, Abindranath's young girl was most probably
a Hindu woman, but Jasimuddin's Shaju is buried in a
grave. It should also be borne in mind that while it is
possible that Muslim women might also embroider
figures, most Muslim women would not. Despite this
discrepancy—or perhaps Jasimuddin was using poetic
licence here—the poem is a fairly accurate reflection of the
intimate relation of Bengali women to the kantha, that is,
until newer ways rent the tradition.

After the kantha revival, it was almost inevitable that
Jasimuddin's poem would influence the course of kantha-
making and that Shaju's kantha would be replicated in
actual embroidery. At Skill Development for
Underprivileged Women, the artist Surayia Rahman
designed two kanthas that might be Shaju's kantha
narrating the story of her life. Scenes from Jasimuddin's
poem illustrate the two pieces, A Tale of Two Villages and

the Field of the Embroidered Quilt. It should be pointed out, however, that these two pieces—like the other pieces done by SDUW—are not true kanthas. The material is new silk material rather than cloth taken from old saris or *dhotis*. The stitch too is not the running stitch characteristic of the kantha, but the Kashmiri filling stitch. Nevertheless, Surayia's work has been influenced by the kantha, in particular Jasimuddin's poem about the kantha. Surayia has, therefore, in a way, returned Jasimuddin the compliment that he paid the kantha. Jasimuddin, inspired by the kantha, immortalized the kantha in his poem, and Surayia, inspired by Jasimuddin's poem, immortalized his poem in her art. In more ways than one, therefore, our rural poet has become part of our kantha tradition.

Small floral motif in *chatai*

Old Threads for New

Kanthas were originally made from old cloth : sari, *dhoti*, *lungi, kapa*—the traditional dress of the women of Rajshahi and Rangpur, consisting of two coarse pieces of cloth, one used in *lungi* or sarong fashion, the other worn over the shoulder in sari *pallu* or *anchal* fashion. Newer kanthas tend to use new cloth, usually unbleached cotton, but occasionally soft silk. There was also traditionally another type of quilt that used new cloth, at least for the top layer: the *sujni* of Rajshahi.

The type of the cloth used for the kantha has often determined kantha type and motif or stitchcraft used. At Rajshahi, for instance, where traditionally the thick *kapa* was used, kanthas tended to be thicker. Of course, it was not only the *kapa* that determined the thickness of the kantha. It was also the type of climate that Rajshahi had, the type of life-style enjoyed by people of the region. Rajshahi suffers extreme heat in summer, extreme cold in winter. People of Rajshahi, like the people of North India, use the *charpai*, a wooden string bed which can be pulled out into the cool night air. For this string bed, a thick kantha was both cooler than a mattress and more comfortable. On the other hand, a thick kantha was also protection against the extreme winter cold.

The thickness of the kantha has, on its part, also affected the style of embroidery. Fine stitches can be taken where the cloth used is fine and where the several layers of cloth are still soft enough to permit diminutive stitches. The thick Rajshahi kanthas do not permit fine stitching.

Nor do they allow for a variety of stitches or motifs. Instead, thick stitches, in repetitive patterns, help create the thick, rigid kanthas that seem more like North-Indian *khes,* than the soft Bengal kanthas.

In addition to these traditional Rajshahi kanthas—called *lohori* kanthas because of the wave-like (Persian *lehr,* wave) motif and stitching associated with them—Rajshahi has also been associated with two other types of quilts : the *sujni* and the "carpet" kantha, both of which used new red *salu* for the upper layer. The bottom layer of the *sujni* used white *addhi,* light white cotton material. In between these two layers was a thin padding of cotton. One *pau,* that is about 8 ounces or 250 grams, was sufficient for this padding. Occasionally old cloth was used for the inner layer, but for a marriage *sujni,* new cloth was always used. From the *sujni* the "carpet" kantha developed. Like the *sujni* it used new red *salu* for the upper layer, but instead of using cotton padding, it used cloth for the inner layer as well. The *sujni* used a fine back stitch, generally in white, to cover the surface in arabesques and floral designs. The "carpet" kantha used coloured threads to embroider geometric or floral motifs in cross stitch.

Apart from the Rajshahi *sujnis,* kanthas made of *lungis* also were coloured. Kanthas made from *lungis* were, however, generally simple kanthas, put together with a minimum of stitching. What we now know as *nakshi* kanthas were not, as far as I know, made from coloured materials.

With the kantha revival, however, we can see changes in the material used. Most new kanthas today that are made to order are made of new cloth. Where attempts are made to keep close to the tradition, unbleached white cotton is used. As this cloth is somewhat thicker than old sari material, only two layers of cloth are used. Occasionally, however, silk is being used. In fact, the "kanthas" made by Skill Development for Under-privileged Women use exclusively silk for the upper layer.

However, other organizations like BRAC and Kumudini too are occasionally using silk as well.

In addition to white material, however, many handicraft outlets are commissioning kanthas made with bright surface material to cater to changing tastes. Usually designed and planned with an eye on a foreign or sophisticated clientele, the total colour scheme is planned—thus avoiding the often garish effect of the red "carpet" kanthas which used brilliant greens and blues on red *salu*.

Traditionally, threads were drawn from sari borders. However, at Rajshahi, where embroidery was heavy and a lot of coloured thread was necessary, new yarn was used. It is interesting to note that the embroidery at Rajshahi was so heavy that both cloth and yarn were weighed before being given to the needlewoman. When the finished kantha was returned, it was weighed again to see that no yarn had been stolen.

The type of yarn used for embroidery has also influenced the colours of the kantha. In traditional kanthas using old threads drawn from sari borders, colours were limited to red, black, blue and white. Newer kanthas, on the other hand, employ a wide range of colours. The colours of a traditional kantha, apart from being limited, also tended to be muted. The saris had been through several washes, resulting in soft, faded tones for the coloured borders from which threads were drawn for kantha work.

Most writers on the kantha comment on the predominance of black and/or blue and red. Kramrisch, for instance, notes that these must have been the original colours. She suggests that kanthas containing considerable amounts of green and yellow are composed of a variety of stitches pointing to a later date.[1] Black and/or blue and red are the colours of the Rajshahi *lohori* kanthas as well, though the *pan* kantha—the Rajshahi *lohori* embellished with the betel leaf motif—uses green instead of blue or black and red.

1. "Kantha," *Journal of the Indian Society of Oriental Art*, Vol.7, p. 54.

It is possible that the earlier kanthas used these few colours because others were fugitive. But even today an older woman stitching a kantha tends to prefer the traditional colours, saying, "Annya rangulo phute na," other colours do not show up so well. However, apart from availability of colour and the effect of the different colours, it should be remembered that colours too possessed symbolic meaning. In *alpana* designs, as well, we may see the predominant use of three colours : red, black and white. Nirad C. Chaudhuri, for example, in *Autobiography of an Unknown Indian*, speaks of the use of brick dust, charcoal dust and rice powder for red, black and white respectively.[1]

White, red and black are the respective colours of the three virtues or *gunas, sattva, rajas* and *tamas*, that is, purity, passion and darkness as Radhakrishnan notes. But white, red and black are also the colours of water, fire and earth. "By the union of Sat or being with the three elements of fire, water and earth, all the varied manifestations of the world are produced. The red colour of fire is the colour of *tejas*, the white of *apas* and the black of *anna ... apas* is water, *anna* is earth."[2]

Did the Bengali needlewoman of the past consider all this when she was threading her needle? Perhaps no, but the old archetypes must have been present in some dim recesses of her ancestral memory. And as she embroidered a kantha, mingled with her own hopes and fears, she embroidered a prayer for unity and harmony of the world around her.

The new kanthas that have emerged after 1978-79 have attempted to revive some of the older forms and colours. The red cross stitch kantha, while not quite disappearing, has given way to the traditional kantha with more muted tones. Differences, however, may be seen in the kanthas designed by the various organizations. Thus the Aarong kanthas, while generally using red and blue and black

---

1. Nirad C. Chaudhuri, *Autobiography of an Unknown Indian* (London, 1951).

2. Radhakrishnan, *Principal Upanishads* (London, 1953), p. 452.

threads on a white background, are not averse to using pinks, maroons, yellows and greens. At the same time, they use coloured material as well, such as red or black for cushion covers. The Aarong kanthas generally tend to be bright. On the other hand, while Kumudini also uses bright coloured threads for small articles like spectacle cases and purses, Kumudini kanthas generally use muted colours, particularly shades of green and blue and brown. The attempt at muted colours is deliberate. It is an attempt to replicate the effect of the older traditional kanthas which, however, it should be remembered, used muted polychromes rather than the muted monochromes used by Kumudini.

Thread drawn from old sari borders is no longer used for kanthas. Instead, rayon yarn is used. The first experiments with kanthas used coloured cotton yarn, the same yarn that was used in weaving. Market demand for a slightly " shiny" kantha has perhaps caused this change. Chemical dyes are used for dying the yarn in bright colours; Kumudini uses vegetable dyes for its muted shades.

The kantha revival in West Bengal, particularly within the last three years, has attempted to replicate traditional motifs and stitches. Yarn used for embroidery is, however, embroidery yarn.

Making A Kantha

Traditionally at least 5-7 saris were needed to make a full-length kantha. Today old saris are being replaced by new cotton material. As this material is thicker than the material of fine old saris, two layers of cloth are sufficient, one for the top, one for the bottom. Full-size kanthas, generally 5 feet by 6 feet, necessitate that pieces of cloth be joined to give the required width. In the Rajshahi *lohori* kanthas, one often finds a narrow red or blue border running down the length of the kantha, testifying to the *kapas* that have been joined to make the kantha.

After the cloth has been joined to give a sufficient width, the layers of cloth are spread on the ground, one on top of the other. This process is the work of several women. The cloth must be smoothed out so that there are no folds or creases either on the surface layers or the lower ones. Weights are placed on the edges to keep the cloth down while the kantha is at this stage. Mohammad Sayeedur notes that thorns from date trees are used to pin the four corners down. In traditional kanthas—which were not meant to be framed as wall-pieces—the edges would then be carefully folded in and stitched. During all this time the kantha must be kept flat on the ground to prevent the layers of cloth being displaced or wrinkled. After the four edges have been stitched, two or three rows

---

1. "Nakshi Kantha Art : A Folk Art of Bangladesh," *The Bangla Academy Journal*, Jan.-June 1992 : 3.

Latifa Begum: Working on a border

Latifa Begum: Taking the last few
stitches in a kantha

Perfecting kantha skills

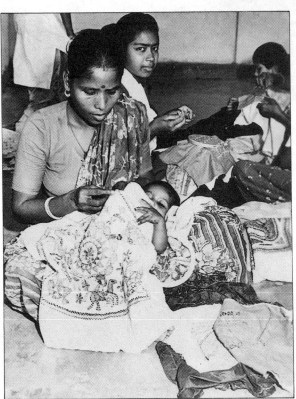

Kantha makers at Kumudini

Checking for flaws at Kumudini

of large stitches are taking down the length of the kantha
to keep the kantha together. It is also probable that these
lengths of stitches acted as guide lines for motifs and
decorative borders—especially in kanthas where the
whole field of the kantha seems to be divided into panels.
Once the kantha has been put together in this fashion, it
can be folded and kept away to be stitched at leisure,
alone or together with other women folk.

While it is a matter of conjecture how women
traditionally embroidered kanthas, one may assume that
when designs were not drawn on to the cloth, the
needlewoman would tend to embroider certain focal
points first and then the filling motifs. When the
predominant feature of the kantha was the central motif,
this would be done first. Corner motifs would follow and
then other motifs around these focal points. This is why in
most kanthas, despite the seeming haphazard nature of
the motifs, there is a sense of order and harmony. The
stitches used to fill motifs in older kanthas were variations
of the running stitch. Thus the *kaitya*, the *chatai*, the kantha
stitch, or the darning stitch picked out the motif from the
rippled white background. The darning stitch could also
take a variety of shapes. Thus it could be in miniscule
stitches, creating a pointillistic effect of dots ; it could be an
interwoven stitch to flatly cover the entire motifs ; or it
could be a thick pattern of close ribs. The background
stitching would go round and round the motifs before
moving out and merging. The effect of this manner of
working the kantha tended to almost mould the motifs
and cause them to stand out in relief against the
background. In newer kanthas, however, the background
stitching tends to move lengthways and breadthways
without regard to the motifs. Also, where the kantha
maker is not careful to pierce through the layers of
material, the rippled effect is lost. The motifs themselves
in many newer kanthas—specially those worked
commercially—tend to lack the variety of stitches
displayed in the older kanthas.

Transparent figure

While generally most kanthas have used the kantha *phor* or kantha stitch for background stitching—thus creating the characteristic ripples of the kantha—in the "kanthas" made at the Skill Development for Underprivileged Women the background stitching has been the darning stitch proper. The reason for this change was to create a smooth surface, rather than a rippled one. (Writers who, following Kramrisch, still speak of the kantha stitch as being the darning stitch should examine the effect of the two different types of stitching. The darning stitch creates a smooth surface, whereas the kantha stitch, if worked closely enough, will always produce ripples.)

Originally, kantha makers did not draw motifs or scenes onto the quilt. Whatever they wished to embroider was first outlined with needle and thread. Occasionally, not satisfied just with an outline, the kantha maker started to fill in a design. Some very primitive effects are created by this manner of working. For example, the scene of a rider on a horse or an elephant often depicts a transparent rider. One understands that the needlewoman first outlined the horse or the elephant and filled it in, and then embroidered the rider. Modern kanthas occasionally replicate this effect deliberately.

Many *bostanis* or *baytons*—wrappers for clothes or other precious articles—are, apart from a central motif, composed entirely of border patterns based on sari borders. One imagines that the outer edge would serve as a guide for the borders which run parallel to the outer border. When the needlewoman continued to work these borders and then came to the central motif, the kantha tended to get bunched up in the middle. Some otherwise very fine kanthas may be seen with this characteristic puckering. However, when the needlewoman seems to have embroidered the central motif before proceeding all the way to the centre, the kantha surface is smooth.

In the Rajshahi *lohori* quilts, the outer edge served as a guideline for the design, with the kantha maker using her

Transparent figure

needle and thread to work the outline of the wave or diamond motifs that predominate in this type of kantha. There was also a very simple *lohori* where the stitches fell into parallel ridges so that the entire surface of the kantha is marked out in alternating lines of red, white and black/blue ridges. In the *lohori*, work would necessarily proceed from one end of the kantha. In the "carpet," *sujni*, and *lik* kanthas, however, needle and thread alone are not sufficient. In the "carpet" and *lik* kanthas, a wooden block with parallel lines would be used to mark out the material with squares. Cross stitch in the case of "carpet" kanthas and *lik* designs in the case of *lik* kanthas would then be worked. In the *sujni* as well, wooden blocks were used to print the central design, overall motifs and border patterns before the embroidery could begin. These wooden blocks are being replaced today by patterns drawn in tracing paper. The designs are pricked out and the designs "printed" on the cloth with laundry blue that has been liquefield with kerosene oil.

Transparent figure

Batuas and *gilafs*, small purses and cases for the Quran, were made from square kanthas. After the kantha was stitched, three corners were brought together in envelope fashion and the edges joined. To the corner left unstitched a long tassel was attached which served to bind the *batua* or *gilaf*.

Traditional kanthas tend to be somewhat uneven in shape. The needlewoman did not use a frame to stretch the kantha. Hence the manner of working, as well as the puckering effect of the kantha *phor*, tended to "shrink" the kantha. Occasionally the centres of square kanthas suffered the most, bunching up in the middle. To counteract this unevenness and bunching effect, some organizations today are using embroidery frames to stretch the kantha while it is being worked. Particularly at SDUW, where a smooth effect is desired, all work is done in frames. Most other organizations, however, allow the women to work freely, in traditional fashion. At the SDUW after the "kantha" is completed, a further smoothening and evenness is achieved by stretching the "kantha" while wet on a wooden frame.

Lohori kantha from Rajshahi

Most writers on the kantha speak of old thread used for kantha work, but it should be noted that where there was considerable use of thread, sari borders did not always prove sufficient. Hence new yarn was also used. In Jessore and Rajshahi, for instance, yarn—called *pheti* in Jessore and *pheri* in Rajshahi—was used. A number of strands were used at a time. In Jessore the strands were left as they were, but in Rajshahi the strands—usually about five in number—were twisted into one thick thread by means of a *taika*. The *taika* has a groove through which the strands pass. The *taika* is then twisted, and the thicker thread collected at its rounded end. The thick thread and the close stitching in the *lohori* kanthas produce the characteristic ridge-like texture. In the thinner Jessore-type kanthas, the fine stitches produce a ripple effect in the texture of the cloth. The stitches, however, are small, and one is not aware of the thread at first glance.

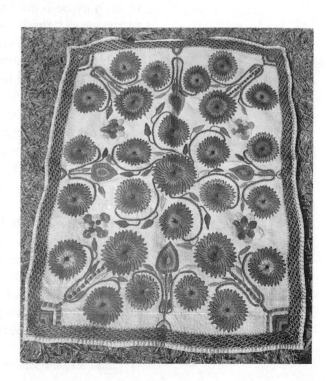

Kantha with floral motifs

Influence of Religion and Folk Belief on the Kantha

Religion and folk belief have been some of the strongest influences on the kantha. Folk belief and superstitions, for instance, have influenced choice of material. The kantha is made of rags—the Sanskrit word *kontha* means literally rags. Now anyone who has visited Indian shrines knows the magical function of rags. In the fretted doorways of the shrines of *pirs* or popular saints, or tied to the branches of trees, may be seen hundreds of rags, symbols of hundreds of prayers. Rags have been used for another purpose as well, that of warding off the evil eye. To the primitive mind, in agrarian societies, the gods of nature are thought of as jealous, ready to snatch away a precious life. To keep a precious life safe, one has to practise deception. By wrapping a loved one in rags one shows the gods that one does not care. "The patchwork quilt, a collection of tatters, guarantees immunity from black magic, protection and security, as do even the rags themselves when offered to the gods," says Kramrisch.[1]

But the kantha has another meaning as well. It is made not just from rags but from the rags of a woman's old sari. An old sari is soft, as soft as the kantha will be when it is made, as soft as the arms in which one would like to hold the loved one safe. Far away from home, the kantha becomes the symbol of one's wife or mother. When Rupa dies in Jasimuddin's poem, it is with the quilt his wife has made wrapped around his body.

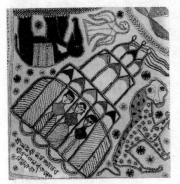

Rath

---

1. *Unknown India: Ritual Art in Tribe and Village* (Philadelphia 1968), p. 67.

The influence of religion and folk belief has worked in other important ways: Firstly, to create different traditions of kantha art, Hindu and Muslim, iconographic and non-iconographic. And secondly, to create different types of kantha articles owing to the different life-styles of the two religions. At the same time it should also be noted that, despite the obvious differences between kanthas of the two different religions, there was one great similarity which resulted from the fact that Hindus and Muslims in Bengal came not only from the same roots, but dwelt in the same land, subject to the same vicissitudes of fortune, the same vagaries of nature.

After the kantha revival of the early eighties, the religious differences are being eliminated. Thus women from Muslim backgrounds are also engaged in embroidering kanthas with motifs which have distinct associations with Hindu mythology and folk ways. Similarly, Hindu women are engaged in embroidering kanthas which are distinctly Islamic in tone. However, an examination of the kanthas traditionally belonging to the different areas of Bangladesh will reveal how kanthas have developed differently among different religious groups.

Kanthas from areas where the predominant culture was Muslim, like at Rajshahi, have developed differently from those where the predominant culture was Hindu as, for example, at Jessore. Thus Rajshahi kanthas have geometrical motifs; Rajshahi *sujnis* have floral motifs, scroll work, and the arabesques and flourishes typical of Islamic art. In Faridpur and Jessore, alongwith floral motifs, there are animal and human motifs as well. Furthermore, in addition to human representations, kanthas embroidered by Hindu women often represent Hindu deities. Lakshmi, Durga, Radha and Krishna were commonly represented. Many of these deities were associated with animals and birds. Thus Lakshmi may be accompanied by an elephant. In one the finest extant specimens of kantha work, Lakshmi is seated in a circle of dancing figures and is accompanied by an elephant. There is also the figure of an owl, associated with Lakshmi, embroidered in the kantha. The lion is associated

Tree-of-life

with Durga. The *rath*, the chariot of Vishnu or Jagannath, was also a popular motif in Hindu kanthas. Some Hindu motifs, however, seem to have become so associated with kanthas that they lost all association with Hinduism and were embroidered by Hindu and Muslim alike. The lotus, for example, the solar motif, even the "S" symbol of Lakshmi's footprint, seem to have lost their religious overtones and were embroidered by Muslim women as well.

Muslim women did not entirely shun representations of human forms. Thus, in a kantha purchased by the National Museum from Sakhawat Moral, there are human figures and fairy heads in addition to birds and animals. However, it should be remembered that motifs with decidedly Hindu or Muslim overtones and associations would not be used in the same manner as those that had lost these meanings; *raths* would not be embroidered in a Muslim kantha, nor a mosque found on a Hindu kantha. The strictures against iconographic art—plus the lack of exposure to representational art—must have induced Muslim women to favour *par* or border designs and floral motifs. It is only now, after the kantha revival, that irrespective of religion, kantha makers are embroidering whatever designs are being given. As Musammat Rabeya, a kantha maker from Pathalia, Jamalpur, said to me, "Kantha banatam. Hati, ghora banatam na." We would make kanthas, but we would not embroider elephants and horses. She pointed out that the women of Jamalpur had started to embroider animal and human figures after BRAC had taught them to do so.

It should be noted that the Muslim kantha maker perhaps did not always consciously avoid human representation. The Hindu woman is surrounded by depictions of the human form—which the Muslim woman is not. In her daily rituals, in her visits to the temples, the Hindu woman is overwhelmed by these depictions. The crude form of the Hindu deities made by the village artisans juxtapose the exquisite stone and metal statues of the temples. The Hindu devotee cannot avoid being influenced by these forms. Kanthas embroidered by

Gopis pleading with Krishna to return their clothes

Fairy figure. Note the ridged effect of the embroidery

Hindu woman who have been exposed to temple art thus reflect this influence. Apart from representations of the deities, the Hindu kantha maker also used her knowledge of the human form to depict men and women. There were no strictures against nudity, and an adept kantha maker from Faridpur has embroidered nude *gopis* pleading with Krishna on the tree top to return their clothes. In another kantha from Jessore, bare-breasted maidens encircle the goddess Lakshmi.

Apart from the creation of two different traditions of kantha art, the Muslim influence in Bengal also created different kantha articles. The need for a prayer rug created the kantha *jainamaz*. In form and motif the kantha *jainamaz* replicates the traditional woven *jainamaz*, with a *mihrab*—mosque-arch—and even a pictorial representation of a mosque. Similarly, the need to cover the holy book gave rise to the *gilaf*—the envelope-like kantha. The Muslim tradition for communal eating also produced the *dastarkhan*—the long spread for an eating place.

Religious influences have therefore had a distinct impact on kantha work. However, despite these differences, it should be noted that perhaps more important than these obvious differences are the similarities of the impulses that created the kantha.

The most important of the religious influences was not that of Hinduism or of Islam, but of folk belief and magic. In a land dependent on the vagaries of nature, propitiation of natural forces becomes an important part of the lives of the people. It was this very important fact that syncretized, if not religion, at least, folk belief. In rural Bengal, particularly, we see how closely Muslim folk ways resemble Hindu folk ways. In a marriage ceremony, particularly, we note this syncretism. Thus, while the Muslim marriage ceremony is based on the *Sharia* and is basically a social contract where the man takes a woman as his wife on payment of a certain sum of money known as the *meher* or dower, the ceremonies preceding the actual marriage ceremony are similar for Muslims and Hindus alike. Thus the *lagan* or *hulud* ceremony, with the bride being smeared with turmeric and medicinal herbs and spices, followed by a ritual bath, as well as the ritual articles that are laid out on the occasion—the fish, the *durba* grass, the banana sapling—are similar for Hindus as well as Muslims.

In an agrarian community, all religious differences were wiped out in the one great religion of nature and harmony with nature. That is why even when we talk of religious differences and the effect these had on the kantha, we must remember that existing side by side with these differences was also a great similarity. Men and women have been very close to nature in Bengal. Their lives are governed by natural forces and their social life too is guided by the seasons. This close association between nature and human beings is reflected in what we may call, for want of another name, folk magic.

Now folk magic has, from earliest times, been related to folk art. The earliest examples of art—the cave drawings—were made not to beautify the walls of caves, but to ensure that the hunt was successful. Writers of early art are unanimous in pointing out the relation between art and magic. As E.O Christensen points out, art has, from the earliest times, given human beings a feeling of protection against the forces of nature. "Art was not the first step in his struggle against insecurity. Man's feelings, his fears came first, they prompted his beliefs, and his beliefs found expression in Art."[1]

This close association between nature, folk magic and art is to be observed in two of the art forms practised by Bengali women: the kantha and the *alpana*, ritual drawings on the ground made with a paste of rice flour—though other ingredients were also used, such as charcoal and brick powder. *Alpanas* were closely associated with *bratas*, religious ceremonies performed in observance of certain vows. There was something distinctly magical about these *bratas*, and the *alpanas* drawn on these occasions served these magico-religious purposes.

Fahmida Majid suggests that the *alpana* had its origin in the magical circle that Rama drew around Sita when he had to leave her. Sita was safe inside this circle. Ravana, who had come to abduct Sita, knew that unless she ventured out of this circle he had no power over her. Disguised as a yogi, Ravana persuaded Sita to step outside the circle. Once she did so she was in his power.

Mohammad Sayeedur points out in "Loukik Chitrakalar Alpana" that *alpanas* are closely related to nature worship and appeasement of a cruel god and prayers for plenty. Tapan Mohan Chatterjee also points out the association of *alpanas* to nature. Whether we call the *bratas* magico-religious ceremonies or semi-religious ceremonies, they are mainly concerned with appeasement of the forces of nature and a celebration of nature. Thus *bratas* were celebrated to observe the change of the seasons, to celebrate the harvest, to pray for rain. They were also observed to pray for the well-being of husband, father, son. A brief list of the different *bratas* will give an

---

1. *Primitive Art* (New York, 1955), p. 53.

idea of the different occasions when *alpanas* were used—and therefore explain how these *alpanas* became associated with different prayers and vows. The seasonal *bratas* included the *Bhaduli brata*, celebrating the goddess of the rains, the *Maghmandal brata* celebrating the cult of the sun god, the *Lakshmi brata*, performed in Autumn, celebrating the harvesting of the new rice. The *Toshla brata* invoked prayers so that fields might become plentiful. In addition to these seasonal *bratas* there were prayers for the well-being of loved ones. The *Bhaduli brata*, for example, also prayed for the well-being of father, husband, son. Marriages inspired other *bratas*.

The *alpanas* drawn for these *bratas*, as well as for birth and marriage ceremonies, often have magical import.[1] It is therefore interesting to note the traditional motifs that would be drawn in *alpanas*. These include lotuses, creepers, animals, anthropomorphic figures, trees, heavenly bodies, footprints, and material objects desired by devotees. *Alpanas* for the well-being of male members of the family include motifs of rivers, tigers and boats, suggesting that by enclosing these within the magic circle the devotee was ensuring the safety of her loved men. Now many of these motifs may be seen as common to both kanthas and *alpanas*. In addition, the traditional configuration of the kantha also resembles that of *alpanas*. In *Naksha*, Sayyada R. Ghuznavi has an illustration of a *Sejuti brata alpana* depicting a central lotus inscribed within a *mandala* or circle. Boats, ornaments, the sun and moon, a palanquin, all figure prominently in this *alpana*.[2] It is not therefore wrong to assume that the same motives that inspired the *bratas* and the *alpanas* also inspired the kanthas. Kramrisch, for example, points out that thematically the art of the kantha is an enriched textile version of the art of the *alpana*, with its magic purpose being enhanced by the textile symbolism of its material.[3] In both the *alpana* and the kantha, the women of Bengal

---

1.   Tapan Mohan Chatterjee, *Alpona* (Calcutta 1965) p.1.

2.   *Naksha: A Collection of Designs of Bangladesh* (Dhaka, 1981), p.572.

3.   *Unknown India: Ritual Art in Tribe and Village* (Philadelphia: 1968).

propitiated the gods and goddesses of nature, and prayed to them for the things close to their hearts: the safety of hearth and home, the well-being of their husbands and sons, harvests of plenty, fertility.

The kantha was stitched for a new-born child, for one's husband, for a grown-up son, for one's daughter to take when she got married and left her home for the home of her in-laws. It was also made, as Manada Sundari's kantha in the Gurusaday Collection reveals, for an honoured father. Colour, motifs, over-all designs were not only ornamental but also symbolic. The mother or grandmother embroidering a kantha for a girl to take with her to her new home would embroider lotuses, fishes, leaves, a winnowing fan, symbols of plenty and fertility. But she would also draw with needle and thread combs and mirrors, a vermilion pot, a *kajal-lata*, or container for lamp-black with which women line their eye-lids. These would be symbols of a married woman. At the same time she would add horses and elephants, symbols of material wealth. Like the primitive artist hunter, she would be "capturing" these objects for the loved one for whom she was making the kantha. And much later, when this child was a mother or grandmother, she too would portray the very same objects for another girl-child.

The *brata alpanas* have given way to decorative *alpanas*; Hindu and Muslim girls alike decorate *alpanas* without any thought of the earlier inspiration behind these *alpanas*. Similarly, Hindu and Muslim women embroider kanthas without a thought that these traditional motifs were not meaningless decorations. Nevertheless, what remains, despite all the changes, is that *alpana* and kantha are women's art, and art, that, with changing circumstances, is being increasingly usurped by men. But it is perhaps not surprising that the finest of kanthas today are still the work of women.

Kantha Stitches

The earliest and most basic of the numerous embroidery stitches to be found in kanthas is the **running stitch**. The predominant form of this stitch in the kantha should be called the kantha *phor* or **kantha stitch**, not the darning stitch. Stella Kramrisch was, perhaps, responsible for designating the form that the running stitch takes in kanthas as the darning stitch: "The technique is that of darning."[1] Following Kramrisch, many writers have referred to the kantha stitch as the "darning" stitch. Thus, Rustam J. Mehta speaks of the different stitches used in the kantha, "the commonest and most typical being very small darning stitches."[2] The darning stitch, however, it should be noted, is an "interwoven stitch." Mehta himself describes how this stitch is worked as follows :

> The needle is run along the cloth, taking up small areas of the cloth at intervals. Correctly, the space between each row should be the same as the length of the stitch, the stitches in each row alternating with the preceding and following row.[3]

Now, anyone who has closely observed the stitchcraft of the kantha will notice that there is no interweaving, nor do the stitches in each row alternate with those of the preceding row. If this had been the case, there would not

---

1. "Kantha," *Journal of the Indian Society of Oriental Art*, Vol.7 (1939), p.36.
2. *Handicrafts and Industrial Arts of India* (Bombay, 1960), p. 115.
3. *Handicrafts*, p.117.

have been the ripples so characteristic of the kantha. This is, of course, not to deny that the true darning stitch may be found in the kantha, but this is in minute proportions to the kantha stitch. Kramrisch seemed to have realized her mistake. Thus, in *Unknown India : Ritual Art in Tribe and Village* she notes, "The stitches are of the simplest kind, the running stitch being not only the main but also the most ingeniously employed."[1] Kramrisch points out that the intricate uses to which the running stitch was put in the kantha appeared to be the invention of the kantha embroiderers.

The principal of the kantha stitch is that minute areas of the cloth are covered by the stitches. The spaces between the stitches are larger than the stitches themselves. When the second row is taken, it is parallel to the previous row, but the stitches fall slightly behind or move slightly forward instead of alternating with the stitches in the preceding or succeeding rows. It is this manner of working that produces the rippled effect, the wavy ridges between the stitches.

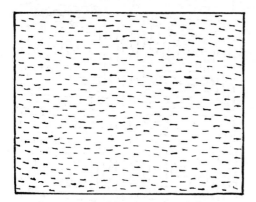

The darning stitch

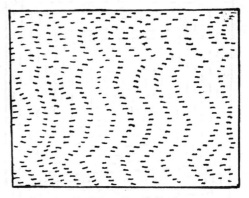

The kantha stitch

1. *Unknown India*, p.67.

When kantha stitches are taken around motifs there is still a tendency to parallel rows, but each row curves with the motif at its centre. This manner of working around a motif often creates an almost sculptured effect, as Kramrisch notes, with "an effect of modelling of its own kind on the textured surface."[1] The very surface of the material undergoes a change. As Perveen Ahmed points out, "The patterns flow and swirl, the entire work assuming an organic live quality."[2]

Occasionally, however, the field of the kantha is worked more regularly, even when using white yarn on a white field. Instead of proceeding in only one direction, the needlewoman works a small square at a time. The square is worked from the outside edge inwards. As the worker proceeds round and round the square, each row of stitches that is taken is parallel to the outer edge. When one square is finished another is worked next to it in the same manner. In this way there are both square motifs and diamond shapes. As Kramrisch points out in *Unknown*

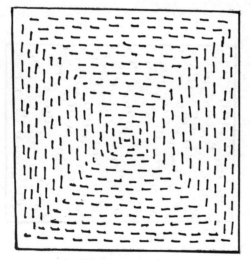

Working a square

Patterns that move and change

---

1. *Unknown India*, p.67.
2. "Kantha : The Embroidered Quilt," unpublished article.

India, the patterns do not remain static, but move and change before our eyes, "the speckled textural effect of the stitches . . . leads the eyes in more than one direction."[1]

The kantha stitch is only one form that the running stitch takes in the kantha. Thus running stitches may be long or short, alternating with those in the preceding and succeeding rows, or bending slightly forward. Each manner of working results in a different appearance altogether. Several of these patterns have been given different names. Some of the most common forms that the running stitch takes in the kantha, apart from the kantha stitch, are the *chatai* or *pati* stitch, the *kaitya*, the *lik*. Along with these, almost every known embroidery stitch is also used in kanthas. One way of dating kanthas may be by examining the use of other embroidery stitches. Earlier kanthas used the running stitch; later ones resorted to a variety of stitches. As Kramrisch notes, "by the middle of the [nineteenth] century, the embroidery stitch is more frequently resorted to than earlier."[2]

Chatai [3] **or pattern darning.**[4] This stitch is also referred to as the *pati phor*,[5] both the names being derived from the resemblance of this stitch to woven grass matting. In this form the stitches are placed closely parallel to each other. The effect of such embroidery often resembles that of the satin stitch—perhaps one reason why many writers frequently refer to the use of the satin stitch in kanthas. It is only by turning over the kantha that one realizes that the satin stitch has not been used. In the satin stitch, "The stitch is worked from one side of the shape to the other, generally slanted at an angle. The needle takes an equally long stitch on the underside so that this is a stitch which eats up a large amount of thread."[6]

---

1. *Unknown India*, p.67.
2. *Unknown India*, p.68.
3. The term *chatai* was used by Begum Salima Ahmed of the Kushtia Mahila Samity.
4. Alison Liley, *The Craft of Embroidery* (London, 1961), p.53.
5. Kantha makers in Jamalpur used this term.
6. Alison Liley, p.53.

In the *chatai*, the worker makes closely parallel rows of running stitches, the rows and stitches both being parallel to each other. The areas covered with embroidery on the surface of the kantha are bare on the reverse. Not only is there a minimum of thread wasted, but the work proceeds at a faster rate than in satin stitch embroidery where a minute portion of the embroidery is worked at a time.

A flower embroidered in satin stitch proceeds slowly as one petal is worked at a time, but a flower done in *chatai* grows quickly. In working with the indigenous stitch, the kantha maker works spaced running stitches around the flower. Not only is the running stitch the most basic of stitches, but also one which allows the whole flower to almost spring into being at once. Even where the final effect of a flower perplexes us as to whether the satin stitch or the *chatai* has been used, a glance at the back of the motif will always reveal the difference. A flower worked in satin stitch will appear the same on the reverse as well, whereas a flower worked in *chatai* will have a complementary design on the reverse.

Some characteristic kantha motifs are embroidered using the *chatai*. Leaves, flowers, the *chakra* or wheel, the *kalka*, the betel leaf, all these are embroidered very quickly by means of this stitch. The final effect belies the simplicity of the stitchcraft.

There appears to be another version of this stitch which resembles *phulkari* work of the the Punjab. In this form the

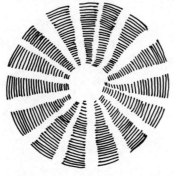

Chakra or wheel in *chatai*

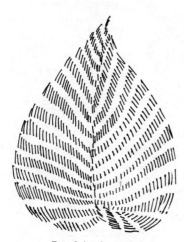

Betel leaf in *chatai*

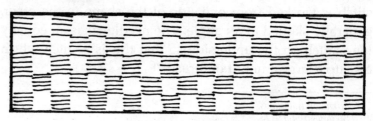

Chatai or pattern darning

space between the stitches is as small as possible, producing an almost matted effect. One difference between this manner of working and that of the *phulkari* is that the latter is limited to embroidery producing angular effects, whereas the former is used for a variety of shapes.

The Rajshahi or *lohori* stitch may be applied to the pattern darning or *chatai* prevalent in Rajshahi kanthas. Whereas in the normal *chatai* the space between the stitch might be almost equal to the stitch itself, in Rajshahi kanthas the stitches are always smaller than the spaces between the stitches. This manner of stitching, plus the thick yarn used in the embroidery, results in the parallel ridges of the Rajshahi kanthas.

In Rajshahi the final effect of the stitching resembles weaving more closely than it does needlework. The ridges created by the manner of stitching are rigid and regular. Coloured as well as white yarn is used so profusely all over the entire field that there is almost no separation of stitch from material, or motif from background in the Rajshahi kantha. At Rajshahi, the wave and the triangle are favourite motifs, but they are so worked as to merge with the entire field of the kantha; they do not remain separate as the motifs elsewhere do.

The *kaitya*,[1] or bending stitch. In this form of running stitch, the stitches are taken in closely parallel rows. Each stitch, however, moves slightly forwards. The whole line

Kalka in *chatai*

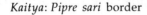

Kaitya: Pipre sari border

---

1. This term was also used by Begum Salima Ahmed of the Kushtia Mahila Samity.

seems to bend, the name of the stitch being derived from this effect. Borders such as *pipre sari* and *bicche par* are worked very quickly using this stitch. In the same way, motifs can also be worked in a short space of time using this variation of the running stitch. The *shostir chinho*[1] or swastika is one instance where this stitch can be suitably employed. In working this motif, the needlewoman outlines the motif with stitches. Using these stitches as a guide line, she works the *kaitya* around the motif, producing a complete *shostir chinho* very quickly. Not only is very little time taken to create this lovely motif, but the effect created is similar to an optical illusion. The motif seems to move before our eyes, giving rise to the feeling that it represents a moving wheel.

Many motifs can be embroidered using either the *chatai* or the *kaitya*. The different form of the running stitch used will create different effects. *Chatai* work is thicker and bolder, whereas *kaitya* work produces a more delicate effect. Occasionally, the *kaitya* is also used for the background stitching. The *kaitya* is sometimes referred to as the Kushtia *phor* or stitch.

The weave running stitch. In kantha borders may be seen the use of the running stitch in a way more characteristic of weaving than embroidery. The stitch varies according to the length necessary, longer or shorter as the design demands. Fairly intricate borders are worked very quickly by this means, as the needle takes the part of the shuttle, weaving in and out of the cloth at required intervals. As Surovi Bhattacharjee notes, the embroidery of Bengal, "is a good example of the point where embroidery becomes indistinguishable from ornamental weaving and leaves one wondering which come first."[2] Nowhere is this truer than for what G.S. Dutt calls "textile pattern kanthas."[3]

Shostir chinho in *kaitya*

Kalka in *kaitya*

---

1. This motif is also referred to as *muchri* or *golok dhanda*.
2. "The Weaver's Art of Bengal," *The Costumes and Textiles of India*, ed. J.B. Bhusan (Bombay, 1958), p.54.
3. "The Art of Kantha," *Modern Review* (Calcutta, 1939), p.460.

As Dutt points out :

> The technique of working these kanthas is that
> of weaving, forms and designs which appear on one
> face are complementary to those on the other and the
> right face is easily distinguishable from the
> reverse face in these kanthas.[1]

The **darning stitch** is also to be found in the kantha. Occasionally used for the field of the kantha, it is more often used for embroidering motifs. Tiny stitches are taken with large spaces in between to fill the surface area of a motif. The effect of this stitch is a dotted, pointillistic one when worked with coloured thread on the white background of the kantha. Kramrisch points out that the stitchcraft of the kantha "yields effects akin to op art but having representational intentions."[2] At the Skill Development for Underprivileged Women, the darning stitch has replaced the kantha stitch for background stitching.

Other variations of the darning stitch are also worked in some kanthas. In one form, a row of large running stitches is worked, the spaces between the rows equalling the stitches themselves. In the next row the stitches and gaps between the stitches alternate with those of the previous row. Closely spaced rows are repeated to produce a large block of colour. The manner of stitching, however, produces an effect of flat ridges rather than the smooth surface that results when the gaps between the stitches are small, as in the "Jessore stitch."

The **Jessore stitch**, another variation of the darning stitch, is so called because of the embroidery done exclusively with this stitch on saris at Jessore today. But this stitch is also often found in old kanthas. In this form of working, the stitch is longer than the space between one stitch and the next. Rows of stitches are taken close to each other, so that the final effect is of a solid area of colour. The underside of the kantha has a dotted effect because of

---

1. "The Art of Kantha," p. 460.
2. *Unknown India*, p.68.

the minute stitches taken on the reverse of the cloth. This filling stitch is today being replaced by the Kashmiri stitch which can be worked more rapidly.

The **threaded running stitch** is a popular one in the newer kanthas. In this form of stitching, a number of parallel rows of spaced running stitches are taken. The stitches are equal in length to the spaces between the stitches. Depending on the pattern wanted, the stitches either parallel or alternate with those of the previous row. When the required number of lines have been worked, the cloth is turned and the needle weaves in and out of these rows of stitches. Depending on the manner of threading the rows of stitches, different patterns emerge.

Detail of Lutfunessa Begum's *jainamaz* showing use of *lik phor/anarasi, kaitya, chatai,* chain, and kantha *phor*

The *lik phor,* [1] as it is called in the Rajshahi area, is also known as the *anarasi* and *ghar hashia*. This stitch has been called the **Holbein stitch** by Liley. The *lik* stitch is a spaced running stitch, but the final effect belies this. In working this stitch, a number of parallel rows of running stitches are taken. The stitches, the spaces between one stitch and the next, and the spaces between the rows of stitches are equal. Depending on the effect desired, the rows of stitches parallel those of the previous row, alternate, or are a combination of parallel and alternating rows. After the required number of rows have been worked, the kantha is turned, and rows of running stitches are taken to join the previous rows. Different patterns emerge from variations of this stitch.

The *lik phor* in Jessore and Faridpur is used along with other stitches. The *lik* kanthas of Rajshahi, however, use only this stitch throughout. Furthermore, in Rajshahi either white or green yarn is used to embroider the *lik* pattern on red *salu*. The stitches are large and bold. Elsewhere, the stitches tend to be smaller and are worked in a variety of colours, thereby producing a result often quite different from that produced by this work in Rajshahi.

---

1.   This term was used by members of the Chapai Nawabganj Kalyani Sangstha.

Detail of Jessore kantha showing a *rath*

Detail of Jessore kantha with Gaja Lakshmi, the goddess being bathed by elephants

Jainamaz from Bogra embroidered by Lutfunesssa Begum.
Approximately forty years old.

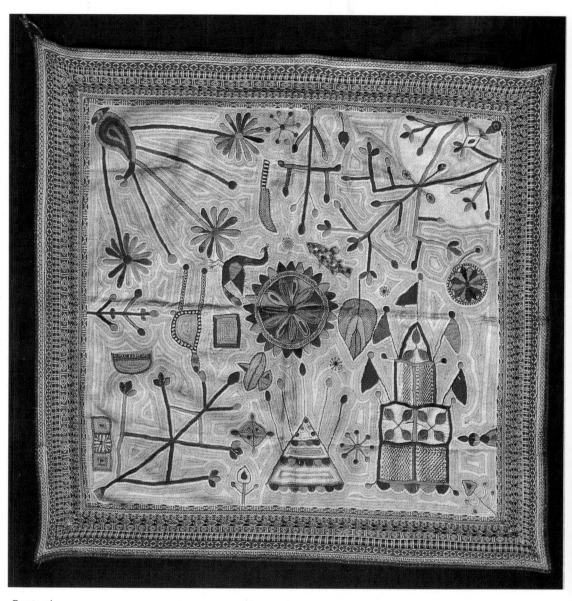

Bostani

While the running stitch, in its different variations, is the basic kantha stitch, almost all other stitches known may be found in kanthas. Some of these stitches suggest a North Indian influence, others European influence.

One of the most popular stitches, particularly in the SDUW and Kumudini kanthas, is the **Kashmiri stitch.** The Kashmiri stitch, as the name implies, is the stitch used in Kashmiri shawls. While not indigenous to Bengal, it is found in kantha embroidery. It shares with other filling stitches the name of *bhorat phor.* This stitch produces the effect of three stitches, but is really a combination of two. A large stitch is taken and then a second small one is taken in the middle to hold the stitch down. If the area to be covered is large, large stitches are taken and then held down by two or three stitches. The Kashmiri stitch is a very suitable stitch to embroider large areas where solid colour is wanted. While large motifs worked in the Kashmiri stitch do not, at first glance, appear very different from large areas worked in other filling stitches, there is one form of Kashmiri embroidery which stands out distinctly. In a number of kanthas may be seen *kalkas* embroidered in a manner very similar to   *kalkas* in Kashmiri shawls. In this form of embroidery, a petal is finished in two or three large stitches and then outlined with two large stitches in a contrasting colour.

While a double row of running stitches is often used to outline motifs, the **stem** or *dal phor* is occasionally used to do so, especially in the newer kanthas. The stem is also sometimes used to fill a motif, producing an effect of solid colour.

The **arrowhead,** composed of two straight stitches meeting at an angle, is used in various ways. It is a quick way to fill motifs which are then neither heavily embroidered nor left without embroidery. It is also used to produce a variety of border patterns, either alone or combined with other stitches.

The **herring bone** is not very common in the Rajshahi or Jessore areas, but is often used in Rangpur and

Jamalpur. Together with other stitches, it helps create a number of delicate looking borders.

The **satin stitch** is also seen in the embroidery of the kantha, but generally for foreign motifs rather than indigenous ones. It should be pointed out, however, that when the satin stitch is used in the kantha for foreign motifs there tends to be an incongruity because of the clash between traditional and foreign motifs. On the other hand, the satin stitch is used successfully in some very typical kantha motifs, and because of the beauty of the motif itself, this blending fits into the kantha tradition.

The **buttonhole stitch** is rare, but occasionally forms the edge of smaller kanthas and is often used ingeniously to embroider *kadamba* motifs.

The *bahkya* or **back stitch** resembles machine stitching, and is the stitch employed, even today, to stitch garments by hand. In this stitch the needle is brought out of the cloth a stitch length ahead of the stitch worked. The needle is then taken back along the line and again brought out of the fabric a stitch length ahead. While the back stitch is occasionally used to outline motifs in Faridpur and Mymensingh kanthas, it is most closely associated with Rajshahi *sujnis*. It is a very appropriate stitch for embroidering the curving outlines of the sensitively drawn floral and leaf motifs.

The **cross stitch** is, like the back stitch, occasionally found in kanthas other than those made in Rajshahi, often combining with other stitches to produce a variety of border patterns. It is, however, most prominently found in the Rajshahi cross stitch kanthas. The cross stitch is the latest stitch in the kantha repertory and, though not quite merging with the kantha tradition, kept the tradition alive when the original form had disappeared from public view. The cross stitch is called the *tin phor* in Chapai Nawabganj because three movements of the needle are necessary to complete the stitch. A variation of the cross stitch, known as the "Gujrati stitch," is being used increasingly in kantha embroidery, particularly on saris and dresses.

The older kanthas often use a variety of embroidery stitches, as Kramrisch points out, but the finest of old kanthas wrested a variety of effects from a dexterous manipulation of the running stitch. The Crafts Council of West Bengal has, for the last four years, been examining the old pieces available in the Indian museums and attempting to replicate their rich variety and ingenious effects.

Different Kantha Articles

While kanthas generally denote quilts used as wrappers, all articles made by quilting old cloth may also be referred to by the same generic name. However, depending on the size of the kantha and its purpose, we may divide kanthas into various articles, each with its own specific name.

Kanthas for use as spreads and coverlets are referred to as *sujni* kanthas by both Dutt[1] and Kramrisch.[2] Manada Sundari, in her dedication of her kantha, refers to it as *sujni*. *Sujni*, which comes from the Persian word *sozni*, is also commonly used instead of kantha in the district of Murshidabad and in Bihar. But in Bangladesh, *sujnis* are generally associated with a distinct type of quilt and are therefore considered separately from the kantha, though the term *"sujni* kantha" may be used for kanthas used as coverlets. Both *sujnis* and kanthas, however, serve the same purpose. Kanthas vary in thickness depending on the climatic conditions under which they will be used, but sujnis are generally of the same thickness. Again, *sujnis* are worked in basically the same pattern, but kanthas vary from the ordinary to the ornate. Thus, for daily use, a kantha might be very simply quilted, with small or large stitches depending on the amount of time on the maker's hands. For giving away to a loved daughter or son leaving home, a kantha might be patterned or covered with motifs and scenes.

---

1. "The Art of Kantha," p.458.
2. "Kantha, " p.36.

In order to distinguish between ordinary kanthas and embroidered ones, the term *nakshi kantha* is used for the latter. Occasionally, the phrase *phul kantha* is also used to describe embroidered kanthas. At Chapai Nawabganj, the term *kantha* refers to embroidered quilts; the term *gadla* is used for roughly stitched ones. With the popularity of Jasimuddin's poem, the term *nakshi kantha* has become synonymous with embroidered quilts. Kramrisch does not speak of *nakshi kanthas*, being content with the word *kantha*.

Kanthas, or *sujni* kanthas, for use as coverlets, measure about 5 feet by 6 feet.

Thicker kanthas, meant for use in winter, are often referred to as *lep* kanthas, the word *lep* being a mutation of the word *lehaf* or cotton padded quilt. As many as seven saris, for instance, might go into the making of a *lep* kantha, whereas three to four saris are sufficient for a thinner kantha. *Lep* kanthas are also somewhat larger than ordinary kanthas, measuring about 5 1/2 feet by 6 1/2 foot. Even when *lep* kanthas are embroidered, the embroidery tends to be simpler than on kanthas used as spreads and coverlets. Often *kalkas* are worked in the four corners and occasionally a central lotus is also added.

Ashon kanthas are smaller square or rectangular kanthas used as spreads for *puja*, the Hindu prayer ceremony, or for eating special guests or a bridegroom. They are among the most exquisite of all kantha work, containing a wealth of motifs and pictorial representation.

Jainamaz, or Muslim prayer rugs, are also made in kantha work. While some are fairly simple, others reproduce the traditional designs of prayer carpets with a floral border and a mosque where the forehead touches it in *sijda*.

A number of small kanthas were also associated with the palanquin. The *palkir topor* was placed on top of the palanquin and the *khat* kantha where the passenger sat.

The *bayton* or *bostani* was a square kantha meant for keeping books or other valuables. Even today, Bengali women tend to wrap up their valuable silk saris in a piece of cloth before putting them away in the almirah or closet.

The *arshilata* was a small rectangular kantha used for wrapping toilet articles such as a comb and *arshi* or mirror. It had a tassel at one end so that the articles could be rolled up and tied.

The *oar, balish kantha, balisher oshar* or *balisher chapa* is a small square or rectangular kantha meant to be placed on top of a pillow. Bengalis use hair oil that soils pillows. These kanthas prevented this soiling. Today they have been generally replaced by small towels.

Gilaf

The *gilaf* was an envelope-shaped kantha meant for covering the Quran. Three corners of the *gilaf* were stitched together and to the fourth was stitched a tassel. A smaller version of this was the *batua, durjani* or *thalia* used as a wallet or to wrap betel leaves.

The *dastarkhan* was a long narrow kantha meant to spread for an eating place. It tended to be about 10" to 18" wide. The length varied, depending on the number of persons who were to use it. Like the *jainamaz* and the *gilaf*, the *dastarkhan* is an example of Muslim influence on the kantha.

Children's kanthas range from very small ones for the newborn to larger ones for toddlers. Even those families that had stopped stitching kanthas for any of the above purposes, still stitched them for newborn children and toddlers. Old cloth served two purposes: one practical, the other magical. In its practical aspect, padded old cloth was absorbent and very comfortable for a small baby. Also, because infant mortality was high, the newborn child was neither dressed in new clothes nor were clothes stitched for him before he was actually born. The fear was that new clothes would attract the evil eye and the child would die. If the child were dressed in rags, this would show a seeming neglect and hence no jealousy would be elicited and the child would be safe.[1] With better chances for the

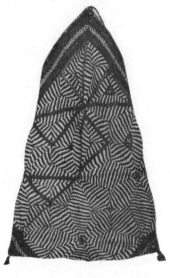

Gilaf

---

1. It is the same belief that causes a much desired child to be named *Pocha*, the rotten one, or *Dukkhu*, the unfortunate.

newborn child, with the ready availability of plastic pants, of towels, embroidered children's kanthas were going out of fashion, especially in urban areas. But with the kantha revival, they have returned.

Small square kanthas known as *rumals* or handkerchiefs are another form of quilting. These small kanthas were often used for covering plates, rather than, as the word suggests, for wiping one's face. A qualifying adjectival phrase should perhaps be prefixed—*bashon dhakar rumal*—to clear up confusion. Mohammad Sayeedur suggests that *rumals* were presented to bride and groom during the wedding ceremony.[1]

Today newer uses are being found for kanthas, with a whole new range of products being made based on kantha work. Thus, among the popular new uses of the kantha are bedspreads, wall-hangings, cushion covers, ladies' purses, spectacle cases, place mats, jewellery boxes, dress fronts, skirt borders, shawls. Many of these items develop traditional uses. Thus a place mat is a modernized version of a *dastarkhan*, as a cushion cover is of an *ashon*. Some are, however, new uses. As, for example, sari embroidery based on kantha work. The most innovative use of the kantha is, however, in the wall-hanging. Whereas the other uses are more or less utilitarian, the wall-hanging is purely ornamental. It has also effected the greatest change stylistically in the kantha.

---

1. "Nakshi Kantha Art," *Bangla Academy Journal*, Jan-June 1992, p.6.

Kantha Motifs

A casual glance at kanthas reveals a plethora of images, of flowers and leaves, of birds and fish, of human figures and huge animal forms, of kitchen utensils and toilet articles. But as we look longer and closer, these sift into some sort of order. As Heinz Mode and Subodh Chandra point out, "the composition as a whole may display a certain type of symmetry . . . . "[1] Even though this symmetry is not always strict, and even though there was allowance for spontaneity, and despite the multitude of motifs and pictorial representations and the appearance of being unplanned, a finely embroidered kantha will always have a focal point. At the centre of most kanthas is a lotus. Around the lotus there are undulating vines or floral motifs or sari border patterns. Occasionally, the outer-most border round the lotus is not circular but square. In the corners of this square, floral motifs or *kalkas* are embroidered, pointing toward the central lotus. The four corners of the kantha also usually have tree-of-life motifs or *kalkas*. There is also an outer border. Often, a number of different *par* patterns are embroidered to create a broad border. The empty space between the central motif and the corner motifs is filled up with motifs ranging from vegetal, animal, and human motifs to agricultural implements and common domestic objects. Symbolic motifs juxtapose scenes from myths or from contemporary life. The kantha

1. *Indian Folk Art*, tr. from the German by Peter and Betty Ross (Bombay, 1985), p.225.

Cross stitch kantha made by Parul in the Bengali year 1359, corresponding to 1952 of the Christian era. The Bengali script translates: Gaya, Kashi, Brindaban are nothing to me/A woman's existence is at her husband's feet.

Kantha made by Johura Khatoon. Approximately sixty years old

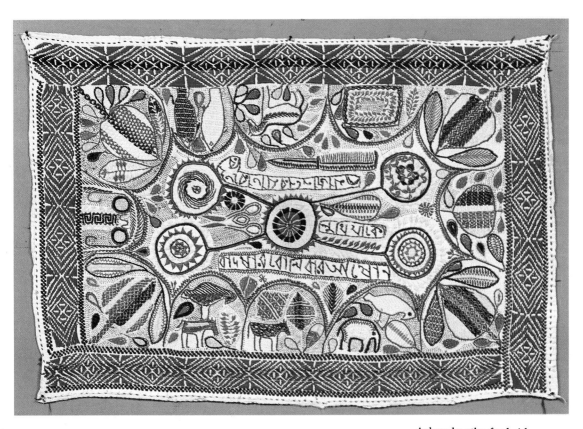

Ashon kantha for bridegroom

Bartan dhakuni or plate cover

Section of *arshilata* from Nilphamari district

Kantha from Manikganj

maker did not try to be representational. Every available
space between the lotus and the corner motifs was filled
with motifs, symbols, and scenes, with size and colour
being guided by the imagination of the artist. Themes
from legends juxtapose scenes of contemporary life, and
both are often permeated with symbolic meanings.

There is a sense of unity and harmony in the kantha
which can also be seen in the blending of motifs belonging
to many cultures and many waves of influence. There are
traditional Indian motifs handed down from the early
civilization of the Indus Valley; there are also motifs
ranging from the farthest western fringes of the Asiatic
continent to its farthest eastern ones. Indigenous motifs

blend with foreign ones and traditional motifs with contemporary pictorial representations.

Thus the central lotus motif is reminiscent of the ritualistic *alpana*. At the same time, the irradiating petals of the *satadal padma*, or hundred-petalled lotus, also resemble the central motifs on the domed ceilings of Persian mosques. At the corners of the kantha are trees-of-life similar to the tree-of-life motif in Persian carpets. *Kalkas*, or paisleys, are reminiscent of Kashmiri shawls, but they might also be drawn from the Chinese symbol of Yin and Yang, the symbol of man and woman.[1]

Kramrisch notes how some motifs in the kantha may be found in other traditions. "The symbols stored in the kantha belong to the primeval images in which man beholds the universe."[2] The solar motif, the lotus motif, the water motif and the earth motif are common to different races and different times. The lotus motif is a ubiquitous one: it ranges from China to Iran and is very much at home in India. The tree-of-life motif is as common in Iran as it is in the kanthas of Bengal.

Water plays a symbolic role in almost all religions; we may note here the baptismal rites of Christianity, *Ganga-snan* or bathing in the Ganges in Hinduism, *wuzu* or ablutions in Islam. It is not surprising, then, that the water motif should be found in the kantha, in the ripples of the surface of the Jessore kanthas, in the fish motif, in the *lohori* design of the Rajshahi kantha, in the *beki* or wave designs of the Jessore border. The sun, too, plays a part in religion : in the fire symbolism of the Zoroastrians, in the early morning prayer of Hinduism. The lotus symbol combines in itself both the sun and the water symbols.

There are also, in the kantha, several motifs that we do not find elsewhere, created as they were from the environment and culture of Bengal. When the kantha maker needed motifs, she looked around her and

---

1. N. Fokker, *Persian and Other Oriental Carpets for Today* (London, 1973), p. 30.
2. "Kantha," p. 53.

embroidered whatever she saw. But she also embroidered what she desired, not only for herself but also for the loved one for whom she was embroidering the kantha. She embroidered the *kula* or the *beri* not only because they were objects familiar to her, but because they were associated with harvests and brimming pots. She embroidered leaves and fish, not only because she lived in a green land crisscrossed with many rivers, but also because she had seen them carved in temple reliefs.

The kitchen utensils, harvesting implements, natural forms, both animal and vegetal, which find their place in the kantha, reflect not only the life of a people but also their hopes and aspirations. As A.K. Coomaraswamy points out, "Indian art is always a language employing symbols valid only by tradition and convention."[1]

In an article on "Kalpavrksa," V.S. Agrawala says, "Indian art conveys its meaning in a distinct symbol language. The lotus, the full vase *(purnaghata),* the svastika, the wheel *(cakra),* the three jewels *(triratna),* and the *kalpavrksa,* part as it were of an alphabet, are being used with perfect mastery as elements of decoration; they have not only invested art, Buddhist and Brahmanic, with endless beauty but also show it as a vehicle of ideas. . . . Their meaning was engrained in the consciousness of the people and the art connoisseur carried within him a subconscious reaction to these symbol forms which intensified his appreciation of an art which was rich both in external narration as well as inward meaning."[2] Bharata Iyer points out the same thing and says that "Employing symbols like the tree, foot print, the wheel and the stupa, Indian art was not using abstract unintelligible emblems that needed expansion. They had grown directly out of the life of the people and their ancient customs, and their significance as symbols was well understood."[3]

---

1. *Introduction to Indian Art* (Delhi, 1969), p. 28.
2. "Kalpavrksa: The Wish Fulfilling Tree," *Journal of the Indian Society of Oriental Art,* Vol. 11, (1943), p.1.
3. *Indian Art: A Short Introduction* (Bombay, 1958), p. 12.

While kanthas employ motifs common to other
cultures, and to all Indian art, there are some motifs that
are common only to the kantha (and to the other arts
which are wholly women's art). This is so because kanthas,
are the work of women, unlike the traditional paintings or
sculpture and even embroideries done all over India by
men. This element may be termed the female element in
the kantha. Among the numerous recurrent images, for
example, are also articles of daily feminine use: mirrors,
combs, betel-cutters, earrings, fish cutters, a *kajal lata*, a
kula, etc. What place do these toilet articles, these kitchen
implements, have in a quilt ?

Very simply, these articles were objects desired by the
women who embroidered the kanthas, just as in the
alpana, as Tapan Mohan Chatterjee points out, these motifs
"are a true picture of the woman's heart—her desires,
fancies and imagination—a great worship of life unlike
the dead ceremonial worship alleged to be based on the
scriptures."[1]

The toilet articles and the earrings are objects used by a
married woman and are thus associated with the married
state. From being actual articles of daily use, they become
symbols of the married state, prayers for happiness in
marriage. In the same way, the palanquin, a common
mode of travel in the past, becomes associated with
marriage. The mother embroidering a quilt for her
daughter would embroider a palanquin, symbolic of the
marriage palanquin that would sometime take her
daughter to her husband's home. In one kantha it is
interesting to note that there are two palanquins. A close
observation will reveal that one contains a female figure,
the other a male; the unknown kantha artist has portrayed
a marriage procession.

The *dheki* or the husking machine and the winnowing
fan are not only articles used in the kitchen or the
homestead, they become symbols of material and
agricultural, prosperity. They become prayers for plenty,
for the fertility of the fields. Apart from these agricultural

------

1. *Alpona* (Calcutta, 1965), p.4.

implements, there are motifs drawn from nature : the tree motif, creepers, birds of different types, horses and elephants. These too are linked to the prayers for prosperity. The fish becomes a symbol of fertility. Most of these are common motifs in kanthas, but sometimes a woman will portray something desired by her for herself or for her husband. An example of this may be seen in a kantha where there are pictures of a bicycle, an umbrella, and a hurricane lamp.

While most of these symbols are naturalistic in form—though not in colour, as colour is quite indiscriminately used, blue leaves, green fish, etc. —there are some symbols which are abstract in form. Lakshmi's footprints, for instance, while originally a detailed footprint as may still be seen in *alpana* designs, is an abstract symbol which is often used in kanthas. In the same way the swastika, or *shostir chinho*, is an abstract symbol quite popular in kanthas. Geometric motifs are popular in the traditional Rajshahi kanthas. We find triangles and diamond patterns predominating. Ajit Mookerjee points out that even geometric motifs may have symbolic meanings. "Geometrical forms dominate the whole range of Indian symbolism, particularly in Tantric designs and formulas."[1] Do the Rajshahi triangular forms convey any symbolic meanings? Are these forms linked to the mountain-water mythology of the Santals and Oraons who inhabit the north-western regions of Bangladesh ?

Since most women desire the same things—personal beauty, conjugal happiness, strong healthy children—almost every kantha breathes the same prayer. But individual differences are to be seen. One comes across a kantha where an unusually artistic woman has embroidered a variety of exquisite flowers. In another the unknown artist reveals her keen observation. She has looked around her and drawn all that she has seen : parrots and monkeys, a train and a marriage procession. She sees nothing incongruous in embroidering a palanquin beside a steaming train. A later kantha artist

---

2. *Tantra Art* (Basel, 1971), p. 13.

Lotus

will, in the same way, embroider traditional motifs alongside the most modern machines, a palanquin beside an aeroplane.

While most kanthas have some initial pattern, none of the finest kanthas proceed exactly according to a set pattern. Traditional motifs are repeated, but in an endless variety of stitches and colours and shapes, and always some touch of the individual is revealed. Some motifs are recurrent, and a brief note on the more common ones is perhaps useful.

The Lotus Motif. The lotus motif is found from distant times, scattered over vast areas ranging from China in the east to Persia in the west. It is to be found in the palace of Darius at Persepolis as it is in the stone columns of Asoka. It is the seat of the gods and goddesses of Hindu mythology, as well as the seat of the Buddha. Coomaraswamy does not think the lotus, along with other such motifs, entered India in the Mauryan period as many writers on Indian art suggest.[1] He feels that these motifs must have been common to pre-Mauryan art. His reason is that if pre-Mauryan had been very different it would have left some of its traces in Mauryan and later art, the Indian artist being a traditional one. It is because of this traditional attitude that the lotus and other Persian motifs could have become so popular, because they must have already been common to Indian art. There was, Coomaraswamy thinks, a common culture, a common early Asiatic art which has left its effects on the shores of Hellas, Phoenicia, Egypt, India and China. The common motifs, of which the lotus is one, must therefore, he says, be regarded as cognates rather than as borrowings.

The lotus motif is associated with Hindu iconography and thus is also popular in the kantha. Generally speaking, it is the divine seat, but it is also symbolic of cosmic harmony and essential womanhood. Thus, as Agrawala notes, the lotus is the divine seat. It is "the

Lotus

---

1. *Introduction to Indian Art*, pp. 1-20.

prime symbol of creation."[1] Just as the lotus floats on the surface of the water, so did the created cosmos emerge on the surface of primeval chaos. The lotus represents the life-giving powers of water but is also associated with the sun, at whose rising it expands and opens its petals, at whose setting it contracts and closes them. The lotus is a symbol of eternal order, of cosmic harmony, of the union of earth, water and sky. As Wajeda Begum of Magura told me, the lotus has its roots in the earth, its leaves and flowers float on the surface of the water, and its opening and closing depend on the sun. It is also a symbol of the recreating powers of life. When the water dries up, the lotus seems to die; but with the rains it springs almost miraculously to life again.

Lotus

The lotus is associated with purity and the goddess Lakshmi. "All of Indian's back country is the dominion of Lakshmi, the goddess of the lotus."[2] And this is no wonder: "She is the embodiment of beauty and splendor, of dignity and glory, of good fortune and wealth, of graciousness and prosperity."[3] She is life itself. The lotus goddess is also the goddess of good fortune. She is the presiding goddess of *dhanya* (paddy) which is wealth in India. She is the goddess of abundance. She is the goddess of the earth.

Lakshmi is embodied in the lotus, but the lotus is more than these qualities; it is also the symbol of the essential woman. As Maury points out, "Though itself of ancient inception, the lotus emblem appears to have been an elaboration of a preexistent design: a floral figuration of the circle, always and everywhere the elementary ideograph of the female organs, subsumed in India by the term *yoni* . . . the lotus has come to represent the ultimate equation of female being and female magic."[4] The break in tradition and the often mindless imitation of older kanthas

Lotus

1. "Kalpavrksa," p.1.
2. Curt Maury, *Folk Origins of Indian Art* (New York, 1969), p.101.
3. Maury, p. 101.
4. Maury, p.101.

result in strange incongruities. Thus, one of the reproductions of a kantha with an image of Gaja-Lakshmi shows instead a nude male in the *tri-bhanga* pose being bathed by elephants.

There are many forms that the lotus takes, ranging from the eight-petalled *astadal padma* to the *satadal* or hundred-

Central lotus with ten petals rather than the more usual eight

Lotus with *kalka* motif

Lotus with *kalka* motif

Drawing based on a kantha in the Indian Museum, Calcutta, showing central lotus with undulating vines and concentric circles

petalled lotus. In the older kanthas the central motif is almost always a fully bloomed lotus seen from above.

The Solar Motif. The lotus motif is intimately associated with the sun. Often the lotus and the solar motifs may be seen together in the centre of a kantha. The solar motif symbolizes the life-giving powers of the sun. "The sun indeed is life," says the *Arthavaveda*. The sun has been one of the first deities worshipped by the earliest peoples, and some remnants of this are still to be found in most religions. With the sun is associated fire, and not only the Zoroastrians gave a symbolic meaning to fire. Fire plays a prominent part in Hindu rites, religious and matrimonial. Easter is a spring festival, replacing a pagan solar festival. The importance of fire and light have not completely faded. A Muslim housewife will light a fire or switch on a light as soon as it is dark.

It must, of course, be pointed out here that the solar motif, like the lotus, has lost its religious overtones and continues to be embroidered in all kanthas regardless of the religion professed by the kantha maker. This is, of course, not the case with the moon motif.

The Moon Motif. The moon motif has religious overtones which make it popular in Muslim kanthas. Usually in the form of a crescent, it is often accompanied by a star. A kantha in the Gurusaday Museum, embroidered by three generations of Muslim women, prominently displays this crescent-star motif. The moon motif with a star is popular in *jainamaz* kanthas.

The *Chakra* or Wheel Motif. The wheel is a frequent symbol in Indian art, both Hindu and Buddhist. It is a symbol of order: "As spokes in the centre of a wheel, everything is established in life," say the *Upanishads*. The world is described as a wheel.

The wheel is a popular motif in kanthas, even when the kantha maker has forgotten what the symbol represents. Its popularity is also partly due to the ease of its embroidery. With the kantha maker simply working in *chatai* around the motif, the design is quickly completed.

Lotus

Solar-lotus motif with Lakshmi's footprints

The Swastika Motif. As a motif in Indian art, the swastika dates back to the Indus Valley civilization. Seals from Mohenjodaro have been found inscribed with this motif. It is often associated with a moving wheel. Kamaladevi Chattopadhaya describes it as being symbolic of eternal motion.[1] It is, to most who embroider it, an auspicious sign, a symbol of good fortune.

Part of the popularity of this motif, as with the wheel motif, stems from the ease of its embroidery. Working in *kaitya*, around a circle, the design is soon completed. Called *shostika* or *shostir chinho*, it is also known as *muchri* or *golok dhanda*. Often its resemblance with the swastika is missing, particularly as the motif has more arms than the usual four. The design is also more curvilinear than the four-armed swastika of the Mohenjodaro seal.

Tree-of-life with human figure

The Tree-of-Life Motif. This motif may also be traced back to the Indus Valley civilization. In *The Flowering of Indian Art*, Radhakamal Mukerjee points out that, "The Indus valley culture has contributed certain permanent elements to Indian culture and art."[2] Of these one important element is that of tree worship and vegetative fecundity. Mukerjee thinks, "It is likely that the Indus people conceived the pipal as the Tree of Life . . . with the *devata* inside embodying the power of fecundity."[3] Even in Buddhist times this cult of trees continued, with the *pipal* being sacred to the Buddha because of the enlightenment he received in its shade. The tree-of-life motif is not peculiar to Indian art, as a glance westwards into Persian art reveals the presence of this motif in the earliest known periods.

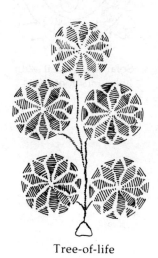

Tree-of-life

In the kanthas, as in the *alpanas*, this motif appears with great frequency. Often it is replaced by a *kalka* or a leaf motif. It is usually to be found in the four corners, representing the four directions.[4]

1. *Carpets and Floor Coverings of India* (Bombay, 1969), p.16.
2. *The Flowering of Indian Art* (Bombay, 1964), p. 34.
3. *The Flowering of Indian Art*, p. 35.
4. Kramrisch "Kantha," p.150.

Kantha with tree-of-life motif. Note the use of *par* patterns for trunk and branches

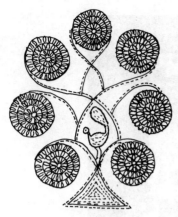

Tree-of-life

Kalka

Yin-yang motif

The tree-of-life motif suggests the fecundity of nature and is therefore popular in an agrarian society dependent on nature. Vegetation has been associated with human fertility since time immemorial. In Indian sculptures may be seen closely entwined bodies of trees and women, as well as representations of trees sprouting from women's navels. In symbolic rites women were married to trees. In Bengal the association of fertility and trees may be seen even today. In the *lagan* ceremony, a banana sapling is still given a prominent place, not only in marriages that take place in the countryside but also in the town.

Vines and creepers play an important part in both *alpanas* and kanthas. They contain the same symbolism as that of the tree-of-life. *Pan* or betel leaves are one of the items carried with the gifts to the bride's house. Marriage *alpanas* include leaf and vine motifs as in the *Mangal charaner alpana.* In kanthas, too, the betel leaf or the *pipal* leaf is often to be found, either attached to undulating vines or in single motifs. A popular non-geometrical motif of the Rajshahi *lohori* is the betel leaf.

The *Kalka* Motif. This is a latter-day motif, dating from Mughal times. It has, however, become very popular in the kantha. Its origins have been variously ascribed. It has been associated with pine trees, the curve representing the windswept pine tops. It has been compared to a stylized leaf ; it has been compared to a mango, whose shape it resembles. Its similarity with a flame has been pointed out.[1] It is also similar to half the Chinese symbol of Yin and Yang, representing the union of man and woman.

The *kalka* is an attractive motif and lends itself to a variety of treatments. It can be worked in *chatai* or *kaitya*, blending in with the other motifs done in a traditional stitch. But often the embroidery of the *kalka* reminds us of its ancestry. For example, it is embroidered with flowers, much in the tradition of Kashmiri shawls. Often the stitch employed is also the Kashmiri stitch.

---

1.   Enakshi Bhavnani, *Decorative Designs and Craftsmanship of India* (Bombay, 1974), p.19.

The Water Motif. This is an almost universal motif and is to be found in the kantha as well. This motif may be found in several patterns. The rippled field of the kantha surface itself symbolizes the rippled surface of water. Borders symbolic of waves such as the *beki* and the *sagar* or *shamuk taga* are popular in Jessore and Jamalpur kanthas. The Rajshahi kanthas are called *lohori* after the wave motif. Apart from these motifs, there are other motifs associated with water: the boat, the fish, and the lotus.

The Mountain Motif. Mountain forms are suggested in both the *lohori* and the *kautar khupi* motifs. In some Rangpur and Jamalpur kanthas, as well, the division of the field of the kantha into diamonds and triangles is suggestive of the mountain. The mountain is a symbol of the contact of earth and heaven.[1] Whether this meaning was intended by the women who embroidered the kanthas is not known, but there is no doubt that the myths and legends of the Santals and Oraons inhabiting this area are concerned with both the mountain and the waters. In their tradition, before the beginnings of this time, the Great Mountain stood alone above the waters. The Great Mountain was not the Creator, but he brought the first man and the first woman together in marriage.[2] In the subconscious mind some of this legend must have been

Sagar or *shamuk taga*

1.   Arthur U. Pope, *Persian Architecture* (New York, 1965), p.12-13.
2.   W.W. Hunter, *The Annals of Rural Bengal* (London, 1868).

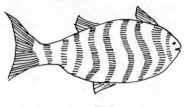

Fish

Makara

retained. The kantha is associated with marriage, and this abstract motif suggests the union of the first man and woman. The *lohori* is claimed to be the oldest type of kantha and it is not surprising that the water-mountain motif should be suggested in the pattern.

The Fish Motif. Fish figure prominently in marriage rites in Bengal. At the *lagan* ceremony, one of the main gifts taken to the bride's house is a large fish. The fish motif appears in both marriage *alpanas* as well as in the kantha.

The reason for the popularity of the fish motif is not only its popularity as an article of food in a land of rivers, but also its fecundity. In an agricultural land many sons are prayed for, and the fish symbolizes this prayer.

The fish portrayed in the kanthas is often a simply drawn fish, but occasionally its appearance is that of the *makara* associated with the statues of religious deities. Thus, apart from being a symbol of fecundity, the fish motif also becomes an auspicious sign, a sign of prosperity.

The Boat Motif. The boat is another popular motif in kanthas. It is not surprising that it should be so in a land crisscrossed by many rivers. But the boat becomes more than a depiction of a normal mode of travel: it becomes associated with all journeys from home. Thus in the *Bhaduli brata alpana*, a prayer for the safety of one's menfolk, the boat figures prominently. As A. Hauser points out, "A picture was both representation and the thing represented, both wish and wish fulfilment at the same time."[1] The drawing of the boat in the *alpana* and the embroidering of it in the kantha would ensure safe journeys for the men one loved, father, husband, son.

After the kantha revival, one particular boat motif seems to have become very popular : the *mayur pankhi* or peacock-prowed boat. Designed for a kantha for

---

1. *The Social History of Art*. Vol.1, trans. Stanley Godman(London, 1952), p.26.

Bostani with what seems to be a fertility motif

Detail of Jessore kantha with tree-of-life motif. Note use of *kaitya* for background embroidery

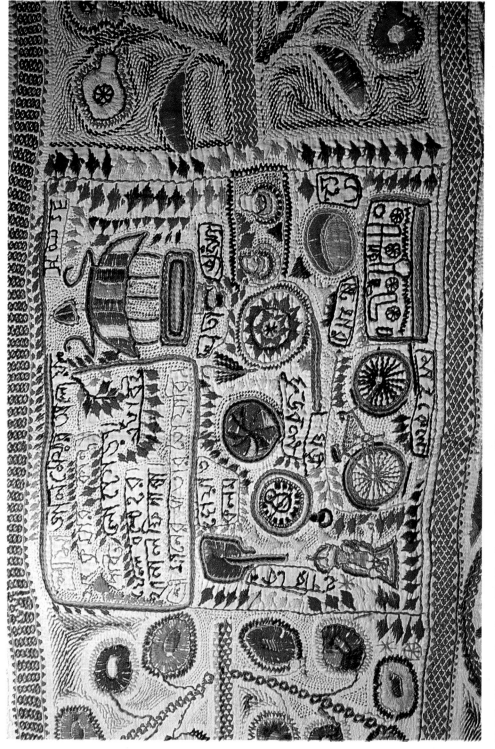

Detail of Jessore kantha with bicycle, earrings, umbrella, hurricane lantern, football, watch.

Modern place-mat

Ashon kantha.

Sonargaon, this motif has been reproduced in countless wall-hangings.

The Footprint Motif. This is a common motif in Buddhist art, with footprints representing the footprints of the Buddha. In *alpanas* and kanthas, however, the footprints become symbolic of the goddess Lakshmi. The symbol has, however, become a traditional one, and continues to be embroidered even when the motif has lost all similarity with a footprint.

The *Rath* Motif. The *rath* is associated with Vishnu or Jagannath. It does not carry the fearsome associations ascribed to it by Europeans. In fact, it is considered an auspicious sign. It is a popular motif in kanthas, especially in those embroidered by Hindu women. Some of these *raths* are very elaborately made, with images of deities and with flags flying. In several, however, the representations hardly resemble a *rath*. Where the resemblance hardly exists, it is perhaps because the kantha artist embroidering the motif is only dimly aware of what she is portraying. She has perhaps seen this motif in a kantha and merely copied what she has seen.

The Mosque Motif. This motif figures prominently in *jainamaz* kanthas, occurring towards the upper portion of the kantha where the forehead touches the ground in *sijda*. It also occasionally occurs in larger kanthas as well.

The *Panja* or Open Palm Motif. A favourite motif among Shias, the *panja* may occasionally be found in Bengal kanthas. Silver replicas of the *panja* are carried in Moharram processions that mourn the martyrdom of Hazrat Imam Hussain, the Prophet Mohammed's grandson. The *panja* symbolises the pentad of the Shias : the Prophet Mohammed himself ; Ali, his son-in-law ; Fatima, the Prophet's daughter and the wife of Ali ; and Hasan and Hussain, the two sons of Ali and Fatima. It has also been pointed out to me that part of the popularity of the palm might stem from the ease of drawing it. Children love to place their hands palms down and trace around them. The palm on the kantha may therefore just be the handprint-signature of the maker.

Lakshmi's footprints

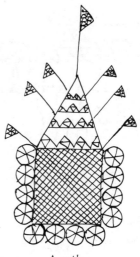

A *rath*

An elephant

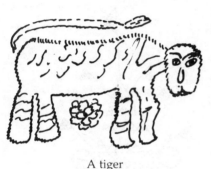

A tiger

A tiger

Agricultural Implements. The *kula* and sickle are motifs common to many kanthas. In an agricultural society these implements are part of every household. But again, these implements become symbolic, being associated with harvests. They stand for the plenty of the fields, for the prosperity of the household.

Animal Motifs. Elephants, horses, peacocks, deer, tigers and monkeys figure in several kanthas. Part of the reason for the popularity of these motifs is, of course, the presence of these animals in a land where animals still lurk in the forests. But more than being chance-met animals, many of them become symbolic motifs in the kantha. The elephant and the peacock become symbols of material prosperity. The peacock, it has been pointed out to me by Mohammed Sirajuddin, is not a local bird. Its presence in the kanthas therefore is suggestive of the receptive mind of the kantha maker, ready to absorb everything. The peacock would, however, suggest the aristocracy who could afford to bring these North Indian birds. Thus the peacock, like the elephant, would suggest material wealth. The tiger in the kantha is often part of a hunting scene ; thus under the power of the hunter as well as of the woman who embroidered the kantha. How, then, could the tiger represent any danger, even if one did meet it in the forest while collecting firewood or fetching water ?

It is also possible, as Hameeda Hossain suggests, that the same motif may have several meanings—some perhaps that the kantha maker was not quite aware of. Thus the horse—which would be associated most directly with material wealth—might also be "a mobile force, symbol of the sun," suggestive of the "coming of the Aryans" or even the "*duldul* from the Moharram story."[1]

---

1. "Symbolism and Tradition of the Nakshi Kantha," Seminar paper, presented at the Folk Art and Crafts Foundation, Sonargaon, February 1983.

A variety of peacock forms

Toilet Articles. Mirrors, combs, earrings, a *surma dani* —a container for antimony used as an eye-liner—figure prominently in large kanthas as well as in *arshilata.* They are articles desired by women for themselves, but they also become symbolic of personal beauty and the marital status.

Kitchen Implements. The *beri* —tongs, the *bothi*—the curving floor knife, the *jati* or betel cutter are other kantha motifs. Apart from being common household items, they represent plenty. They are symbolic of brimming cooking pots and plenty of food in the kitchen.[1] The *jati*, for example, contains the hope that the person who uses the kantha will have plenty of betel nuts to cut, and plenty of betel leaves to eat with them.

The Kantha Motif. The kantha, too, occurs as a motif in kanthas. Occasionally it is a simply embroidered article, but often it is elaborately embroidered with a number of motifs. In this case the embroidered kantha motif becomes a symbol of marriage.

The Palanquin Motif. The palanquin is another traditional kantha motif. Not only does it represent the mode of transport of the past, but it is also associated with marriage, the bride being generally carried in it. The palanquin thus also becomes a symbol of marriage.

Detail of *ashon* kantha.
Note upside-down palanquin

---

1.   When a Hindu bride comes to her husband's home, she is welcomed by numerous rituals. One of these involves a pot of milk full to the brim.

Apart from these traditional motifs in the kantha, almost all of which tell us about the life of the people and their hopes and fears, there were several other motifs that the kantha maker embroidered into her kantha. Whatever she saw, she embroidered into it. Some strange designs are, therefore, also to be found. One kantha, for instance, contains the imprint of the Bombay Dyeing Mills embroidered onto the kantha. Embroidering what she saw, the kantha artist embroidered the world around her. And embroidering what she wanted for either herself or for the person for whom she was making the kantha, she described the inner world of the rural Bengali woman.

Kantha Borders

Most kanthas have some form of a border : either a sari border is stitched on, or a border pattern is embroidered around the kantha. Other kanthas have these borders as their main feature, often so closely parallel to each other that there are no spaces between them. In Jessore, Faridpur and Kushtia, border patterns are often used to ornament leaves or stems.

Border patterns have innumerable designs, the weave running borders being the older and more valuable because they are a repertory of border designs, some of them no longer worked in saris. As G.S. Dutt notes, "in them we find conserved old traditional patterns of border designs of great variety and loveliness which were undoubtedly used in making saree borders in the older times but the use of many of which in the saree borders has been discontinued by the weavers. . . ."[1]

At Faridpur, Jessore and Kushtia, borders are still worked today in weave running, but elsewhere there is a tendency to employ either the threaded running stitch or a combination of various stitches like the cross stitch, the feather stitch and the arrowhead in simple border patterns.

Many of the patterns are traditional and have definite names, but occasionally traditional names are used for innovations as well. Several of the names come from agriculture or from folk beliefs and superstitions. While

---

1. "The Art of Kantha," p.460.

most come from nature, a few — because of the receptive mind of the kantha artist—come from the machines that are increasingly becoming a part of life everywhere.

From agriculture come the names *dhaner shish* and *khejur chhori, motor dana, phul par, jhop taga, anaj taga*. From superstitions and folk beliefs come the names *ta'abiz par* and *chok par*. From water symbolism comes the *beki* or the wave-patterned border. From nature we have *maach taga*. And from the world of machines come the names *wrench taga* and *grafi taga*.

Pipre Sari. This is a border worked in the *kaitya* stitch. A row of running stitches is taken, not only to act as a guide line for the remaining lines but to mark the beginning of the border pattern. Each succeeding row of running stitches is taken parallel to this row, but each line moves slightly ahead of the previous one. The appearance of this border pattern is very similar to a row of moving ants—a very familiar sight when the rains start in Bangladesh. While this pattern is usually worked as a border, it is also occasionally worked in the field of the kantha.

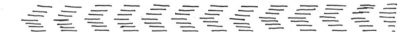

Dhaner shish or *khejur chhori*, the rice stalk or date branch

Dhaner Shish or **Khejur Chhori, the paddy stalk or the date branch**. This border pattern is also worked in the *kaitya* stitch. After a row of *pipre sari* has been worked, the row is "bent" to give the impression of a paddy stalk or date branch.

Bichche Par or **scorpion border**. This is a variation of the above. Instead of one bend, there are three v-shaped bends, the final effect being similar to a stylized scorpion.

Bicche par, the scorpion border

Beki, **the wavy or bent border.** The *kaitya* is worked in wave-like patterns.

Motor Dana **or pea border.** This is one of the simplest of borders worked in the *chatai*. The most common is a row of small squares, suggestive of a row of peas. Small circles are also occasionally to be found.

Barfi **or diamond.** This border in weave running stitch comprises of a row of diamond shapes. The pattern has a number of variations, some because of the distinctness of design, being called by separate names.

The *Chok Par* **or the eye border.** This is really a variation of the *barfi*. The white circle in the centre of the diamond motif, encircling a black circle, creates a strong impression of an eye; hence this name for the border.

Motor dana, the pea border

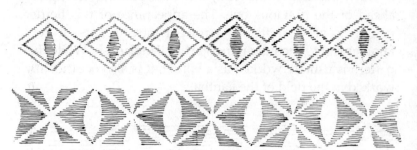

Variations of *chok par*, the eye border

Beki

Ta' abiz par, the amulet border

Kantha from Jessore with tree-of-life motif

Par tola sujni kantha with central lotus

Par tola bostani with tree-of-life motif

Detail of *par tola bostani*

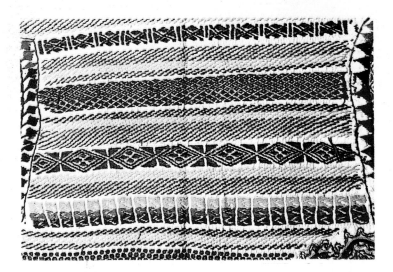

A variety of border patterns

Ta'abiz Par **or amulet border**. This pattern is so-called as it resembles the *ta'abiz* or amulet worn by women in rural areas. It is also to be found in folk jewelry elsewhere in India. It has been pointed out that it resembles the design on the walls of the palace of Akbar's Turkish queen at Fatehpur Sikri and thus it was perhaps originally a Turkish design.[1]

Mala taga, the necklace border

Intricate as some of these design are, it must be remembered that none of them are drawn on to the cloth. The first row of running stitches acts as the guiding line for the best of the border. The sure eye of the needlewoman and her steady hand create these traditional border patterns in the kanthas.

Less elaborately worked borders are often a blending of the traditional running stitch with other stitches. Many of these borders have been given names from objects familiar to the women who have embroidered them. Thus, even when composed of foreign stitches, they have succeeded in blending into the tradition of the kantha.

Moi Taga, the ladder border

The *Mala Taga* [2] is composed of running stitches and the cross stitch. Two rows of running stitches are taken, the stitches being also parallel to each other. The distance between each stitch and that between the two rows is the same. After these two lines have been completed, cross stitches are taken in the spaces between the stitches.

The *Moi Taga* is a variation of this border. The same type of parallel rows of spaced running stitches is taken. After this, however, a row of cross stitch is worked between the two parallel stitches.

---

1. This piece of information was given to me by Bunny Page, formerly of Aarong.
2. The names of these delicate looking borders, many of them in the threaded running stitch, were given to me by kantha makers at the BRAC centre at Jamalpur.

The *Gut Taga* consists of three rows of parallel running stitches. Two cross stitches are worked one on top of each other between two rows of stitches. Leaving the next space blank, the cross stitches are repeated in the space between the next pair of stitches.

Gut taga

The *Chik Taga* is a variation of the *gut*. In this version, rows of cross stitches are worked in all the spaces between the stitches.

The *Nolok Taga* is a combination of three stitches: the running, the cross and the arrowhead. A row of running stitches is first taken. Then a row of cross stitches is embroidered between the stitches. The design is completed with a row of arrowheads.

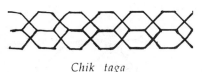

Chik taga

The *Maach Par* is a combination of the running stitch and the herring bone stitch. A row of running stitches is taken. A row of herring bones is then worked. At this stage half a fish is completed. A second row of stitching completes the design.

The *Panch Taga* or *Panch Mala Taga* is one of the simplest forms of the threaded running stitch. Three rows of alternating running stitches are taken. The needle then weaves in and out of the stitches.

Bisa Taga is a variation of the *Panch Taga* border. Two rows of closely spaced running stitches are taken on both sides of the *panch taga* to complete this border pattern.

Nolok taga, the nose-ring border

The *Anaj Taga* is also made up of three rows of alternating running stitches, but the needle takes up different stitches as it weaves in and out of the rows. A pattern similar to a row of beans is the result.

The *Shamuk Taga* is also called the *Sagar Taga,* as it resembles curving waves. Four rows of alternating running stitches are taken as the basis for this border. Interestingly enough, versions of this border occur over distant times. It is to be found not only in the kanthas, but also on Peruvian pottery.

The *Chok Taga* is also worked in the threaded running stitch. Three rows of parallel running stitches form the

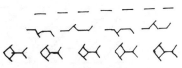

Maach par, the fish border

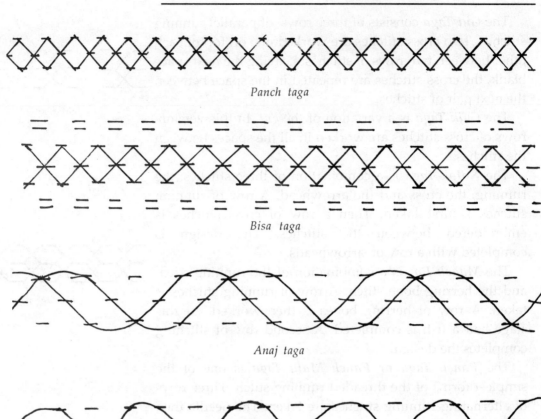

Panch taga

Bisa taga

Anaj taga

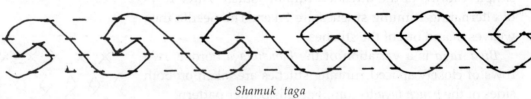

Shamuk taga

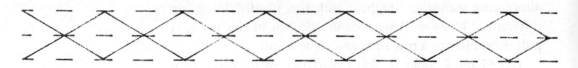

Chok taga

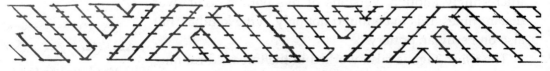

Rens taga, the wrench border

Miscellaneous border patterns

basis for this border. A stitch in the centre of each diamond serves as the pupil of the *chok* or eye.

The **Rens Taga** or **wrench border** is worked on a number of rows of alternating running stitches. Though one does not think of the wrench as a motif for embroidery, the kantha maker does not think it incongruous.

The receptive mind of the kantha artist is revealed in two other borders : the *grafi* —the anchor—and the *kalam* —the pen. In addition to these borders there are numerous other borders without names. Hameeda Hossain and Tofail Ahmed have documented a hundred border patterns.[1] Ahmed prefers these ingenious border patterns to motifs.[2]

The intricate nature of some of these border patterns suggests a close intimacy of the kantha maker with a variety of weaving patterns. It is perhaps not surprising that the most exquisite of kanthas using sari border patterns are to be found in areas associated with the weaving of fine saris. In the late nineteenth century, N.N. Banerjee noted that fine saris were woven at Satkhira, Hooghly, Bankura, Nadia, Pabna, Dhaka.[3] G.N. Gupta mentioned the production of high class saris in Kishoreganj and Tangail.[4] G.S. Dutt noted how *par tola* kanthas, or what he referred to as "textile pattern kanthas," were made by women of the weaver class, particularly in the district of Jessore.[5]

While the most common use of these *par* patterns is to embroider borders, old kanthas also used these patterns ingeniously to embroider motifs. Using simple as well as intricate weaving techniques, the kantha artists

1.   *Survey of Folk Crafts and Documentation of Designs in Bangladesh.*
2.   Personal Communication.
3.   *Monograph on the Cotton Fabrics of Bengal* (Calcutta, 1889).
4.   *The Industries and Resources of Eastern Bengal and Assam for 1907 - 1908* (Shillong, 1908).
5.   "The Art of Kantha," p.460.

embroidered designs into floral or leaf motifs. And occasionally, as Manada Sundari did in her kantha displayed at the Gurusaday Museum, the kantha artists used these patterns to embroider varying designs in the garments worn by the human figures represented in their kanthas.

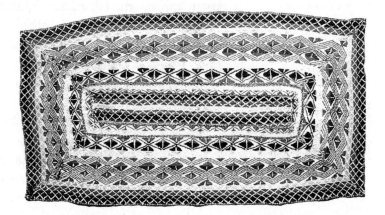

Small *par tola* kantha

Different Types of Kanthas

Embroidered kanthas vary in style according to the material used, the stitch employed and the total design or lay-out of the kantha. According to the stitch employed, kanthas may be divided into four types : the running stitch kantha, the *lohori*, the *lik*, and the cross stitch kantha.

The running stitch kantha is the truly indigenous kantha. Originally always composed of old cloth, it is now-a-days often made with new cloth, usually cotton but also occasionally silk. Borders and motifs are embroidered by means of numerous variations in the running stitch itself, but a number of other embroidery stitches may also be used.

The running stitch kantha may be of two types : *Nakshi* or figured and *par tola* or patterned. Figured kanthas may again vary between motif kanthas and scenic ones. In motif kanthas the interest lies in the motifs which appear to be scattered randomly all over the kantha. There, however, does tend to be a pattern in many such kanthas with a central lotus and trees-of-life in the four corners. In some motif kanthas, the kantha is divided into panels and the panels then filled with motifs. Some kanthas are scenic kanthas with several scenes being depicted : wedding processions, a dance of *gopis*, women with peacocks, a hunting scene, gentlemen of leisure, a boat journey. The story of Radha and Krishna finds a prominent place in a Faridpur *ashon* kantha, as does a marriage scene. In such kanthas the scenes are often focussed around a central lotus motif. In others, the kantha is divided into sections, each section containing a separate scene.

The *par tola* or *sarir par* kantha is a patterned kantha which features designs similar to patterns of sari borders. The *par tola* kantha is of several types and ranges from the simple to the elaborate. *Par* or border designs are worked in a variety of stitches. Older kanthas are usually worked with the weave running stitch, the *kaitya* and the *chatai*, the newer ones with the threaded running stitch and composite stitches comprising two or three different types of stitches.

The simplest type of the *par tola* kantha has a *par* pattern around the edges and a white field in white running stitch. A slightly more elaborate type of *par tola* kantha has some additional *par* patterns covering the field of the kantha. These *par* patterns either run vertically down the length of the kantha or are worked parallel to the outer borders. Other variations have an outer border with an inner border parallel to it. The inner field of the kantha is then demarcated with *par* patterns into diamonds. Occasionally a kantha with an outside border will have four corner motifs, with the rest of the kantha quilted in white running stitches. Some of these kanthas have an interplay of a pattern of diamonds and triangles. In an even more elaborate version of a *par tola* kantha, concentric border patterns are embroidered around a central lotus motif. *Par* patterns or trees-of-life come from the corners to meet at the central motif. Sometimes a few motifs are scattered in the panels, but, with the prominence of the *par* patterns, the interest in the motifs is secondary.

Some of the finest *par tola* kanthas are covered with concentric *par* patterns around a central lotus motif. There is no gap between one *par* pattern and the next, the whole kantha giving the appearance of a woven piece of cloth rather than a stitched one.

The *lohori* kantha is another traditional kantha, and peculiar to the Rajshahi area. According to Mohammad

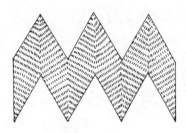

Lohori motif

Kautar khupi

Charchala

Sayeedur, the *lohori* might even be the oldest type of kantha. The name of this kantha is derived from the Persian word "lehr," after the wave pattern popular in these kanthas. It should, however, be noted that this wave pattern is not the only pattern to be embroidered in this type of kantha, the *kautar khupi* or triangle, the diamond and even straight lines being popular.

The *lohori* kantha is made of *kapa* —the two pieces of rather coarse cloth which are still worn by some women of the Rajshahi region. The *kapa* is a white sheet of cloth with borders in red or blue. Often a *lohori* kantha has a strip of this coloured border running down its length, testifying to the material which has gone into its making. Made from a number of *kapas* stitched together, the *lohori* is thicker than the kanthas of Jessore or Faridpur made from saris.

The *lohori* required a large amount of yarn; hence the thread used for these kanthas was not thread pulled from the edge of sari borders but yarn twisted with the help of a *taika*. Closely parallel running stitches were taken with this yarn. Unlike the Jessore *kanthas* where the kantha *phor* produces a rippled texture, the effect of these closely parallel stitches in the *lohori* kanthas is that of regimented ridges. Where coloured thread has been used, the effect is of coloured ridges of yarn, interspersed with white ridges of material. The effect of the stitching is similar to that of weaving, and the patterns appear to have been woven into the kantha rather than embroidered onto it.

Lohori kanthas have neither a profusion of motifs nor of colours. The designs of these kanthas are geometrical and limited to angles and lines. A single pattern is repeated throughout the kantha. Limited colours are used, generally red, blue, black and white. There is a tri-colour effect in these kanthas with the use of red, white and either blue or black yarn. Occasionally the black or blue thread runs out, and the kantha maker continues with whichever colour is available.

The *shoja* —straight or simple kantha—is the simplest of the *lohori kanthas*. Vertical lines are worked into the kantha to produce a pattern of stripes. Tofail Ahmed refers to the *shoja* kantha as a distinct type of Rajshahi kantha known as the *chhop tana*. However, this kantha uses the same stitch as the more popular *lohori*, and may be considered as a variation of the *lohori* rather than a separate type.

The *lohori* or wave motif may be used to cover the entire kantha. Occasionally the lines are broken by vertical lines as found in the *shoja* kantha. Among the other variations of the *lohori* are the *kautar khupi*, the *charchala*, the *aatchala*, the *barochala*.

Aatchala

The *kautar khupi* — meaning pigeon coop— or triangle —and the *barfi* or diamond motif are other popular motifs of this type of kantha. The diamond is stitched in different ways, the manner of stitching resulting in subtle variations. These variations are known by particular names, depending on the number of triangular patterns visible in one diamond. Thus we have the *charchala*, the *aatchala* and the *barochala* , depending on whether there are 4, 8 or 12 triangles visible.

Apart from these geometrical patterns, there is one other motif to be found in the *lohori* kantha—the heart-shaped betel leaf. This motif is generally worked in green yarn, the manner of stitching producing a pattern of white veins where the material of the kantha shows through.

Barochala

A third type of quilt is the *lik* or *anarasi* kantha. At Chapai Nawabganj red *salu* is used for the upper layer, but old cloth for the remaining layers. At Jessore, where the stitch is also popular, old white material is used rather than red *salu*. Coloured yarn is used for the embroidery. Fewer layers of cloth are used at Jessore; therefore the Jessore kantha is softer than the Rajshahi *lik* kantha.

The simplest of *lik* patterns is that of steps. A more attractive pattern is that of the *lik phul*. In this pattern a number of rows of stitches are taken, the stitch in each row alternating with those of the previous row. Then a row of stitches parallels the pattern of stitches in the previous row. The same number of rows are then worked as the preceding parallel rows. After this the kantha is turned, and the rows of stitches joined by lines of parallel stitches, creating attractive patterns.

There are a number of variations of this pattern, each variation having a different name. The names of some common *lik* patterns at Chapai Nawabganj are *lik tan*, *lik tile, lik jhumka, lik lohori*.[1] *Lik* patterns are embroidered all over the kantha.

Lik phul or *anarasi*

Lik   lohori

---

1.   These names were given to me by the late Mrs. Efratunnessa of Chapai Nawabganj.

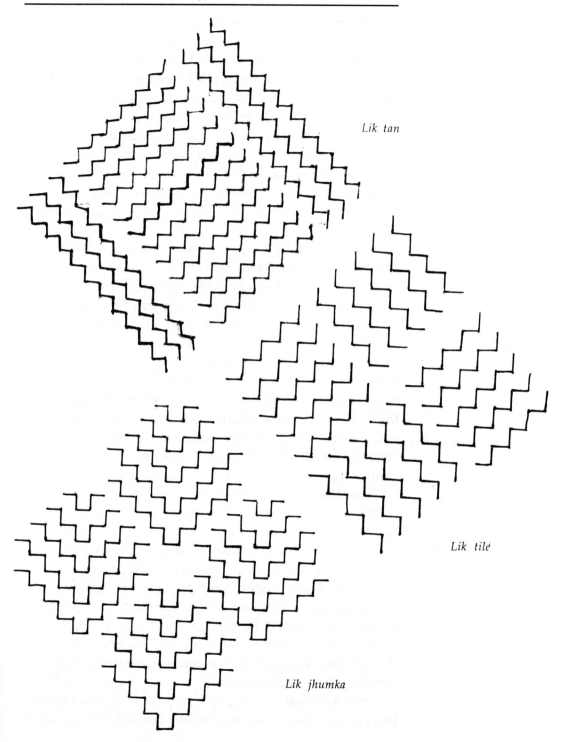

Lik tan

Lik tile

Lik jhumka

Until the kantha revival of the eighties, the "carpet" or cross stitch kantha was the most popular of commercial kanthas. Most cross stitch kanthas are worked on red *salu*, like the *sujnis*. The other layers, however, are composed of old cloth. Some cross stitch kanthas are also found made of white material, but these are much fewer. The origin of the "carpet" kanthas should not be difficult to discover. The stitch is so obviously a foreign stitch that some Englishwoman—the wife of a District Magistrate perhaps—must have helped to create it. From my talks with the women of the Chapai Nawabganj Mahila Sangstha all I was able to learn was that the kantha had been introduced by foreigners. Mrs. Marjina Haq told me that her grandfather had cross stitch pictures embroidered on *do-sooti* material and framed on the wall. These pictures were made in imitation of such pictures hanging on the walls of English drawing rooms. A brief analysis of the term "carpet" used for this kantha might also help suggest its origin. I was told by Sri Aurobinda Ghosh of Kaliganj Babupara that Hindus would stitch *galichas* in jute with threads drawn from sari borders. The needle used was thick. Now the thick needle used for such embroidery— and for stitching woolen garments—is known as the "carpet" needle. It is therefore possible that the carpet kantha originated from a hybridization of these cross stitch embroideries and the *sujni*.

The indigenizing of the cross stitch and its being employed for kantha work resulted in a substitution of local motifs for foreign ones. Usually, the motifs to be seen in the carpet kantha are a delocalized "Indian" type rather than truly Bengali ones. Very popular, for example, are elephants and their *mahouts*, deer and peacocks, in addition to stylized flowers. A fine "carpet" kantha on white material embroidered with delicate cross stitches in the National Museum collection proclaims that a woman's temple is at her husband's feet.

After the kantha revival, the carpet kantha has become less popular, with most people who can afford it choosing

Detail of cross stitch kantha

the traditional kantha over this one. Nevertheless, the carpet kantha is much cheaper than the traditional kantha, and its bright colours make it attractive to local tastes. Hence its popularity continues.

There is a fifth type of quilt: the *sujni*. While it is different from the kantha, the cross stitch kantha and the *lik* perhaps originated from the *sujni*. Hence it might be well to consider it here. The term *sujni* is also used for quilts from Bihar, but the Rajshahi *sujni*—with which this term is exclusively associated in Bangladesh—is different from that of Bihar, which is really a version of the kantha. The term *sujni* appears to be a mutation of the Persian word *sozni* and, apart from this similarity of nomenclature, there is also a similarity of motifs. The

Motifs for central panel

sujni motifs usually consist of undulating floral and vine forms, reminiscent of these forms in Persian art. No animal or human forms are depicted in the *sujni*, nor the domestic implements or harvest tools recurrent in other kanthas. Some of the designs appear to be the influence of the British presence here. It should be noted that village women at Raja Rampur refer to the *sujni* as *Belayeti sujni*, and it is therefore not surprising to find western motifs among the more eastern ones.

While the kantha is made from old cloth, the surface material of the *sujni* is always new red *salu*. The remaining layers of cloth might be old, but occasionally, especially for a marriage *sujni*, the bottom layer is new white *addhi*. A thick padding of cotton is used instead of old filler cloth.

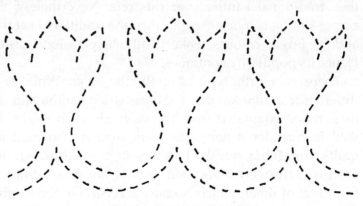

Panchomul motif for *kanha*

Bostani with *satadal padma* or hundred-petalled lotus

Small kantha from Natore

Bostani with *astadal padma* or eight-petalled lotus

The Hunt : SDUW wall-hanging

Miscellaneous border patterns from Rajshahi *sujnis*

The stitch used to embroider the *sujni* is a very fine back stitch, so fine that it appears to have been made by machine. The thread is almost always new white yarn which has been twisted with the help of a *taika*. Occasionally, however, one might come across a few portions of embroidery worked with a different thread, this being occasioned by the lack of white thread or, as generally happens today, because of the influence of the carpet kantha.

In the kantha, the needlewoman traditionally used her needle to draw the outlines of the motifs and border patterns before filling them in. In the *sujni,* however, the designs were always stamped on to the quilt using carved wooden blocks, similar to those used in printing cloth. In every kantha, while there is a similarity of design because of the traditional ways in which kanthas were made, there is always something a little different between one kantha and the next. In the *sujni*, however, there tends to be a similarity of design. A popular design would be handed round the *para* or neighbourhood, and there would be a sameness not only in the *sujni* itself where the same design is repeated, but also in *sujnis* made in different houses in the *para* where almost every family would be related.

Every *sujni* repeats a certain pattern. There is a central panel called a *zamin* round which are a number of border panels called the *kanha*. These panels are separated by two straight lines. In some *sujnis* there is a central lotus motif within the *zamin* as well as corner motifs in the corners of the central panel. Apart from floral forms and leaves, geometrical forms are also popular. The commonest of these are interlacing circles forming a stylized floral motif. Local names for some motifs are *gach* and *panchomul*. Now-a-days the *sujni* borders are being increasingly used on saris embroidered in kantha stitch. Thus there is a blending of both types.

With the kantha revival, the traditional running stitch kantha has come back into fashion, quite displacing the cross stitch kantha. However, certain changes have taken place in the stitchcraft, with the traditional kantha stitch undergoing a change. Kumudini, which was instrumental in bringing back the kantha, perhaps began this process of change as well.

When Sonargaon Hotel commissioned Kumudini for kanthas, Kumudini started training women in kantha work. This training involved the teaching of two distinct stitches : the kantha stitch and the Kashmiri stitch—called Kashmiri *bhorat* or Kashmiri filling stitch. In addition, women were also taught how to embroider *par* patterns in the weave-running stitch. The Kashmiri stitch—perhaps because of the ease and speed with which large areas of the surface can be covered—has become so popular that it is used in some quilts rather than the kantha stitch. In order to distinguish between embroidery using the running kantha stitch and embroidery using the Kashmiri stitch, the terms *nakshi* and "tapestry" are employed. When the Kashmiri stitch is used, the work is referred to as "tapestry" rather than as kantha. The pieces at Skill Department for Underprivileged Women and at Arshi tend to be tapestry rather than kanthas proper. At Kumudini, as well, much of the work done for spectacle cases, for example, is tapestry rather than kantha. However, the Kashmiri *bhorat* is used for large areas of kanthas as well. When the kantha stitch is used in addition to the Kashmiri stitch, the work is still called kantha.

At BRAC centres, workers are encouraged to develop forms of border patterns using the threaded running stitch. The ease of working these border patterns might encourage the use of these patterns by other kantha makers as well in preference to the weave running border patterns based on sari borders. It should be remembered that the kantha is no longer an art preserved in museums, but a craft used for income-generation. The ten years of kantha revival, therefore, are bringing in tremendous changes, changes that we will continue to find in future.

Regional Differences in Kanthas

Wherever there are saris, there are kanthas. Thus kanthas are made almost all over Bangladesh. However, embroidered kanthas are mainly associated with the area west of the Meghna. The area east of the Meghna is traditionally associated with woven, rather than embroidered, quilts. At Sylhet we have the Manipuri type quilt, and in the Chittagong Hill Tracts narrow strips of woven cloth are sewn down the middle to give a wrapper of sufficient width. It is true that Dinesh Chandra Sen described Sylhet as a kantha-making area. Similarly, Jasimuddin has also mentioned Sylhet as a kantha-making area. In fact, the kantha that inspired Jasimuddin to write *Nakshi Kanthar Maath* was from Sylhet. Jasimuddin himself, however, had not seen this kantha. He had only heard that Abindranath had seen a kantha from Sylhet district which a woman had begun after her marriage and had continued to embroider, putting into it all the incidents of her life. "Shilpacharya Abindranath Sylhet jelaye ekkhana kanthar sandhan peyechhilen. Tate ekti meye biye ho'te arambha kore tar sara jibaner ghatana kanthar upar bunat korechhilen."[1]

No kanthas from Sylhet, however, are to be seen in museums. Most people who mention Sylhet as a kantha-making area seem to do so following Sen and Jasimuddin.

---

1. "Purbabanger Nakshi Kantha O Sari," in *Bangladesher Lok Oitijja*, ed. Shamsuzzaman Khan (Dhaka, 1985), p.270.

The popularity of the kantha and its income-generating possibilities are blurring the differences between kantha-making regions and non-kantha-making regions. They are also blurring the regional differences between kanthas. Nevertheless we may still talk about a kantha-making region and a non-kantha-making region. The kantha-making region may again be divided into three distinct areas—though with increasing popularity and production, the same type of kantha is now begin produced in kantha-making centres in Jessore, Kushtia, Kapasia, Jamalpur, Chilmari. Nevertheless, it may be pertinent to note the distinct types, particularly as they still do exist. These types may be divided into Rajshahi, Jessore and Mymensingh, corresponding to the areas with which they are associated. Tofail Ahmed suggests that there are two main types: Rajshahi and Jessore.[2] I would, however, suggest that there are three main types, particularly as despite its similarity with the Jessore kantha, the Mymensingh kantha has certain differences which justify its being classified separately.

Rajshahi Kanthas. There are four different types of embroidered quilts associated with Rajshahi : the *lohori*, the cross stitch kantha, the *lik* kantha and the *sujni.* Each of these is distinct not only from the kanthas made elsewhere in Bangladesh but also from each other. It may be interesting to mention here that each type of Rajshahi kantha uses only one type of stitch throughout. While all the stitches found in the Rajshahi kanthas are to be found in kanthas elsewhere, they are usually combined with other stitches. Of the four types of kanthas to be found at Rajshahi, the *lohori* is the oldest. This kantha is also called the *loria* or *lohira.* The *lohori* is a thick, stiff kantha meant to spread on the webbed bedstead known as *charpai.* The colours are predominantly white, red, black and/or blue. The stitch used is a close running stitch. It is similar to the *chatai* or *pati phor*, but the effect is different as the spaces between the stitches in the *lohori* are larger than the

---

2. *Lokshilpa* (Dhaka, 1985), p. 59.

Detail of Faridpur kantha with Radha-Krishna scenes

Detail of Faridpur kantha with Radha-Krishna scenes

stitches themselves. The close stitching covers the entire field of the kantha, so that the very texture of the kantha undergoes a change. Motifs are few, being limited to the *lohori* or wave motif, the diamond with its variations of the *charchala, aatchala, barochala,* and the *pan* motif. The muted colours of this type of kantha, the lack of variety of motif and design, and the considerable amount of time needed to make it, have gradually caused this kantha to fade in popularity. On the other hand, the "carpet" or bright cross stitch kanthas are more popular and quicker to embroider. Though they have somewhat paled in comparison to the Jessore kanthas, they are still being made, because they are still a bargain. The *sujni* too is still made at Rajshahi especially to give a girl as part of her dowry. Even people who have migrated to other parts of the country will send back to Rajshahi for a *sujni* to give a girl about to get married. However the *sujni* too has become less popular.It cannot, for instance, be used as a wallpiece as the newer kanthas can.

The *lik* kantha uses the *lik* or Holbein stitch throughout. While this stitch is popular in other kantha-making areas as well, in Rajshahi it is used in this type of kantha to the exclusion of other stitches. The *lik* stitch as worked in Rajshahi tends to be larger than that worked elsewhere. Also this kantha, like the *sujni,* uses red *salu* for the surface material.

Jessore-Faridpur Kanthas. Some of the finest of traditional kanthas have been produced in Jessore and Faridpur. The stitch used is the running stitch in its many variations. The Jessore-Faridpur kanthas are made from fine white sari or white *dhoti.* Four saris are sufficient for a large kantha. Generally, threads drawn from sari borders are used to embroider the kantha, but new yarn is also used. Nowadays new yarn is used exclusively. However, unlike the Rajshahi kanthas, fewer strands of thread are used. These strands remain separate, not being twisted into one as in Rajshahi. While both Jessore and Faridpur produce similar types of kanthas, there appears to be a difference between the two. Jessore kanthas are slightly

Exceptionally fine kantha
from Barisal

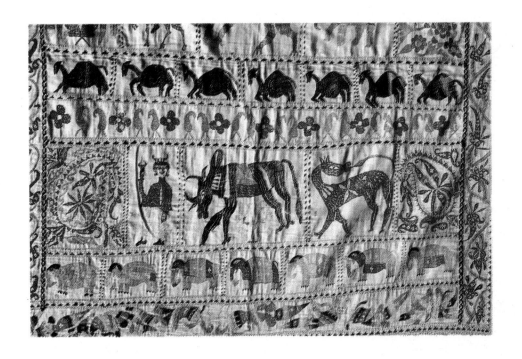

Detail of Barisal kantha depicting human and animal forms

Detail of Faridpur kantha

Par tola bostani

more muted in colour. Even where bright colours are occasionally used in the Jessore kanthas, the areas so covered are small. The stitches in the Jessore kanthas are small and fine, producing a delicate look in the finest of these kanthas.

There are two types of kanthas produced at Jessore : *par tola* or sari border kanthas and *nakshi* kanthas. Some of the finest of border patterns are to be found in Jessore kanthas. Often stems of leaves or trunks of tree motifs are worked in weave running border patterns. While motif kanthas from Mymensingh may look similar to those from Jessore, Mymensingh kanthas do not have elaborate border designs.

In *nakshi* kanthas there is not only a wealth of motifs but also a wealth of embroidery stitches. The usual stitch in these kanthas is a small neat kantha *phor* or ripple stitch. The *kaitya* is often employed, not only for border patterns, but also for motifs and even for background. The *chatai* is used, specially for the wheel motif. This produces a satin stitch effect and often the only way of telling the difference is to see the reverse side of the kantha. The Jessore stitch is used for filling larger areas of colour, but an occasional use of the Kashmiri stitch may also be found. Kashmiri stitches are also used to embroider the *kalka* motif, reminding one very much of the working of this motif in Kashmiri shawls. The chain, the herring bone, the open chain, the zigzag stitch, the darning stitch, an occasional buttonhole stitch for edges, may also be found, particularly in the new kanthas.

Colours employed in Jessore kanthas are red, black, blue, green, yellow and occasionally pink. The total effect of the use of colour is, as has been pointed out, generally quieter than in the Faridpur and Khulna kanthas which the Jessore kanthas resemble. Sayeed Ahmed, for example, notes, that "Exquisite floral designs in subdued colours are distinct in Jessore quilts."[1] Sometimes one come across a

---

1. "Bangladesh Handicrafts," *Bangladesh Handicrafts*, 1974 (Dhaka, 1974), p. 4.

kantha where there are only a few touches of colour. The beauty of such a kantha depends on the interplay of diamond and triangular forms in the white rippled field.

Jessore and Faridpur kanthas are a veritable treasure chest of motifs and scenes. Common motifs are the central lotus, the tree-of-life, the *kalka*, the betel leaf, the *shostir chinho*, the wheel, the *rath*, peacocks, parrots, elephants, tigers, horses, men, women, mythological deities and flowers. Apart from these, domestic articles and farm implements also find their place in the kantha. Toilet articles—the comb, a mirror, a *surmadani*, earrings—are very popular and become symbols of marriage. The palanquin finds a place in the kantha as does a train. Truly scenic kanthas are occasionally to be found. In one such kantha a central figure is surrounded by a circle of dancing women. Beside this group are two *raths*. Another kantha seems to tell a story, beginning with a marriage procession, through a fight with a tiger and a journey by train.

While Faridpur kanthas are similar to Jessore kanthas, a few differences should be mentioned. Faridpur kanthas are more colourful than those of Jessore, both in respect of *nakshi* and *par tola* kanthas. In addition to the colours employed in the Jessore kanthas, there seems to be a fondness for orange which tends to produce a greater vibrancy of colour in the Faridpur kanthas. Also, larger areas of solid colour are to be found in Faridpur kanthas produced by having closely spaced filling stitches.

There are some very fine specimens of Faridpur *bostanis* at the Bangladesh National Museum. These are far more colourful than Jessore bordered kanthas. In these *bostanis* the borders are worked close to each other, around a central lotus or sun motif. There are no spaces between these borders, unlike those in the Jessore kanthas. The effect of these kanthas is more like that of weaving than embroidery.

Khulna kanthas are similar to Faridpur kanthas. Bright colours are used, often verging on the gaudy. The kantha *phor* is used to cover the background and large filling stitches for motifs. The variety of stitches used in Jessore kanthas is absent generally from Khulna kanthas. There are, of course, always a few exceptions. Apart from *nakshi* kanthas, some very fine *par tola* kanthas are also to be found.

Mymensingh-Jamalpur Kanthas. With the kantha revival and the BRAC work in this region, Jamalpur kanthas dominate. Hence it might be better to designate this type Mymensingh-Jamalpur rather than Mymensingh.

Kanthas of Mymensingh and Jamalpur districts are district from those of Rajshahi as well as Jessore. They are colourful and attractive, with both a variety of colours and motifs—and in this way are similar to the kanthas of Jessore. Red, blue, yellow and green are the predominant colours used, but occasionally black and even pink may be found. Vines, the lotus, the sun, the wheel, fish, birds and the *kalka* are frequent motifs. These kanthas may, however, be easily distinguished from those of either Faridpur or Jessore. Large areas of colour are absent in these kanthas, motifs being generally filled with either the kantha *phor* or the darning stitch. Thread is more sparingly used in these kanthas. Again, the embroidery of Mymensingh kanthas is not as fine or delicate as that of Jessore kanthas. Often there is no background stitching, and even the motifs are merely outlined. While Jessore kanthas sometimes come close to sophisticated art, Mymensingh kanthas are generally "folk" art. Large birds perch on dimunitive elephants, unrecognizable horses prance around on spindly legs.

Borders embroidered in these kanthas are generally simple. We do not find the elaborate *par tola* kantha here. Nor are border patterns used to embroider stems as in Jessore or even Kushtia kanthas. Motifs are simply embroidered, and borders are usually based on the threaded running stitch. Some very fine border patterns are to be found; the love of natural forms which appears in motifs elsewhere is reflected in these border patterns worked in the threaded running stitch.

Apart from these three areas, other districts like Kushtia, Bogra, Rangpur, Pabna also produce kanthas.

Ashon kantha from Khulna

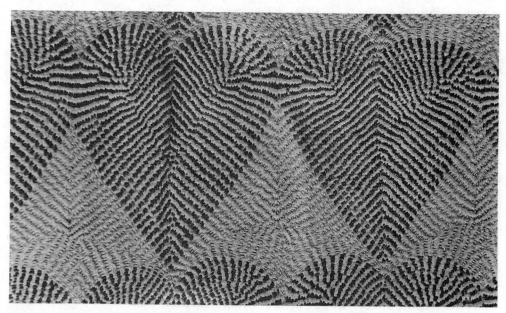

Lohori kantha with betel leaf motif

Many of these kanthas may be seen to have characteristics similar to both the Rajshahi *lohori* and the Jessore kanthas. I would like to designate this type as the **Kushtia-Bogra kantha**. Kushtia-Bogra kanthas have characteristics common to both Rajshahi and Jessore kanthas. Like Rajshahi kanthas they are generally thick, seven saris being used to make a kantha. In the stitching as well they have a hard, ridged effect, similar to that of Rajshahi kanthas. In the Rajshahi *lohori*, however, the stitch is smaller than the space between the stitches. In the Kushtia kantha, on the other hand, the space between the stitches depends on the motif to be embroidered. Apart from the *chatai*, Kushtia kanthas also use the *kaitya,* the kantha *phor* and weave running stitch for border patterns. While the use of these stitches reminds one of Jessore kanthas, it should be noted that Kushtia work is not as fine as that of Jessore, nor quite as colourful as either those of Khulna or Faridpur.

Both *nakshi* kanthas and *par tola* kanthas are to be found at Kushtia. Bordered kanthas are mainly made with a few border patterns either running down the length of the kanthas or parallel to the outer borders. The body of the kantha is worked with the kantha *phor*—much larger than that of Jessore work. The number of motifs used in kanthas is limited. Floral and leaf motifs, the *kula*, the wheel, the fish, the boat : these are common motifs. One motif is, however, striking enough to be mentioned: —the outstretched palm, symbolizing the Prophet Mohammad, his daughter Fatima, his son-in-law Ali, and his two grandsons, Hasan and Hussain.

I would like to designate another type the **Barisal kantha**. These kanthas are usually simply made with a minimum of stitching. The background is rarely embroidered with the rippling kantha *phor*. Instead, fine stitches run in straight lines across the kantha to hold the several layers of cloth together. The motifs are sparingly stitched, large ones being outlined. Borders are simple.

These regional differences are, however, in danger of dying out. With increased training in kantha work, with commercialization and quality control, with designs being giving by designers based on what will sell, it is possible that these differences will soon be wiped out. Nevertheless, it should be borne in mind that while regional differences might be eliminated, differences perhaps will still remain, but most possibly associated with different organizations rather than with regions. Thus we may see three distinct forms of the Jessore kantha today. The SDUW "kanthas," which include those of Surayia Rahman—who was associated with this centre at its inception—are distinct from those of Aarong/BRAC and Kumudini. There is even a feeling that the SDUW "kanthas" are not true kanthas, though they might have been influenced by kantha work. These "kanthas" employ a close Kashmiri stitch to fill in motifs and scenes. The background of the "kantha" is stitched in the darning stitch rather than in the kantha stitch. The SDUW "kanthas" are meant to be displayed as wall-hangings. Therefore all effect of rippling has been eliminated.

The Aarong-Kumudini kanthas are similar to each other, as both organizations have attempted to stay as close to the tradition as possible. Here too, however, differences may be noted. Both Aarong and Kumudini use the running stitch, the *kaitya*, the *chatai* or *pati phor*. In addition, they also use the Kashmiri for a filling stitch. Perhaps Kumudini goes a little heavier on the Kashmiri stitch. On the other hand, the Aarong kantha, which originated from the centre at Jamalpur, tends to favour, especially for borders, the delicate threaded running stitches in many variations. Kumudini kanthas also tend to differ from the Aarong kanthas in their use of vegetable dyes and muted colours for their characteristic kanthas. There is an over-fondness it seems for shades of green, blue, brown, a dull maroon—perhaps in an attempt to replicate the muted shades of traditional kanthas.

Kantha Revival

In Bangladesh, the artists Zainul Abedin and Qamrul Hasan were influential in reviving the traditional arts of Bengal. Hasan's efforts in this direction led him to adopt a distinctive folk style in his art, and also helped in the establishment of the Design Centre at East Pakistan Small and Cottage Industries Corporation—the present BSCIC—which has contributed—though in a much smaller way than it could have—to the revival of the kantha, along with other folk arts and handicrafts. Zainul Abedin's attempts at nourishing our folk art led him to projecting the need for a folk art museum, and led finally to the establishment of the Folk Art and Crafts Foundation at Sonargaon. He also personally collected kanthas—some of the finest of the extant kanthas are in his collection—hoping that some day these would be preserved in the museum. Only a few of the kanthas collected by him are, however, to be found at the Folk Art and Crafts Foundation. The Bangla Academy also contributed, though in an indirect way. Mohammad Sayeedur, a collector at the Bangla Academy, had also been associated with Zainul Abedin in collecting kanthas. When attempts were made, in the early seventies, to revive indigenous crafts, Mohammad Sayeedur was approached and proved immensely instrumental in collecting kanthas. Thus kantha enthusiasts were able to use these as models to develop new kanthas and as displays at craft exhibitions of the traditional arts of Bengal.

Despite the interest of Zainul Abedin in kanthas, the attempts by EPSCIC at producing indigenous handicrafts, and the embroidery of a few   fine pieces, the kantha remained a lost craft until after the liberation of Bangladesh. The kantha revival may perhaps be linked to two factors: a sense of national difference which inspired the resurgence of indigenous crafts, and the need to provide for women left destitute during the war. As Hameeda Hossain notes in "Organising Women's Employment Through Kantha Production," the first attempts at kantha revival took place as early as 1972 with women in kantha-producing regions attempting to make kanthas for commercial purposes. The link between kanthas and commercialization was therefore established early, but the kantha revival did not get under way for another ten years. It should be pointed out that these were not the first kanthas to be made for the market. Earlier kanthas too had often been made against payment. The difference between these earlier kanthas and the later ones was that initially an individual maker would be commissioned to make a kantha. The later products were made by women's organizations for generally unknown customers.

The second step towards the kantha revival was taken in 1974 with the holding of a National Handicrafts Exhibition. It was inspired greatly by Zainul Abedin who had long sought to give due recognition to the indigenous crafts of Bangladesh. The purposes of this first national handicrafts exhibition were described as follows:

> The first national handicraft exhibition organised by an ad hoc committee of individuals, seeks, to:
>
> 1)   introduce folk crafts to the urban world;
>
> 2)   help preserve the existing crafts and improve production;
>
> 3)   project the vast possibility in this field, as well as to
>
> 4)   gain an insight into the problems faced by the artisans in improving their production and techniques.

---

1.   *Bangladesh Handicrafts 1974*, p. 3.

The exhibition came as an eye-opener to many Bangladeshis who were unaware of their own crafts. The success of the exhibition led to the setting up of a permanent craft sales centre. With 2 lakh taka, the Bangladesh Hastashilpa Samabaya Federation began with its outlet Karika, located just across the road from Hotel Intercontinental (at present Hotel Sheraton). Karika was the first organization to attempt to make kanthas on a commercial scale. However, the large kanthas on display tended to be few and far between. Red carpet kanthas predominated. Traditional kanthas were few. On a small scale, there was an attempt to make ladies' purses, place-mats, and dress fronts/panels with kantha embroidery. From 1974-1980 Karika led the revival of indigenous crafts. This success of Karika was unfortunately to prove a setback. The next five years saw rapid expansion and, for the first time, Karika suffered losses. Part of this was due to the strong competition from other similar organizations that had emerged, part due to mismanagement. Karika has not regained its once monopolistic hold on the handicrafts market. However, it has continued to function. One of its best contributions to handicrafts and the kantha is the *Survey of Folk Crafts and Design Documentation*, prepared by Tofail Ahmed, Hameeda Hossain and Mohammad Sayeedur, in 1988. Initiated in 1985, the Survey of Folk Crafts and Design Documentation Project documented over 5000 folk designs from Bangladesh village. Under this project *Nakshamala*—a set of design cards with folk motifs—was produced. The first *Nakshamala* set was *Nakshi Kantha*. (Others were *Nakshi Pitha, Nakshi Pankha* and *Paper Cut Designs*.) These drawings make the rich tradition of the kantha available to everyone.

BRAC (Bangladesh Rural Advancement Committee) began on a low key in 1972—just a couple of years earlier than Karika—but with its more centralized organization it was able to proceed steadily. It was also able to engage the services of several well-paid consultants to develop distinct areas. Thus, BRAC was the first organization to launch the *jamdani* with a big bang in the mid-seventies. After the *jamdani* came the kantha. In 1979 BRAC introduced kantha-making at its project in Jamalpur. With its well-developed marketing strategy, BRAC started producing small kantha articles based on the traditional kantha skills of the Jamalpur area.

It was around this time that the Sonargaon Hotel was being planned. The hotel was to represent Bangladesh in miniature. What could be more Bangladeshi than the kantha? Thus, among the decor the kantha would be included. The management approached Aarong, the handicrafts outlet sponsored by the Mennonite Church Council, but also associated with BRAC and where the BRAC kantha items were sold. Aarong had by now established a reputation for itself as the patron and outlet for Bangladeshi crafts of quality. Would Aarong be able to produce kanthas similar to those in Stella Kramrisch's collection? Aarong had not, so far, done anything as ambitious, but it was willing to give it a try. Involved in the kantha project at this time were Sally Smith, Razia Qadir, Bunny Page—an Indian Parsi married to an Englishman—and Sister Michael Francis—an American nun who had involved herself with handicrafts, first with the successful jute works at Jagaroni, located next to Holy Cross College in Tejgaon, and then with Aarong. It was at this time that the artist Surayia Rahman was approached to design a kantha for Sonargaon. Choosing three designs—a boat scene, a dancing scene and a hunting scene—Surayia Rahman designed a "new" kantha. Razia Qadir, who was mainly designing silk saris for Aarong, also designed a kantha. Razia did not attempt to copy old kanthas. Instead, she sought to capture the essence of rural Bengal and included that most romantic of rural scenes: the marriage palanquin. Both Surayia Rahman's design—copied several times, in different variations—and Razia Qadir's—obliterating the central lotus and focussing on rural Bengal—have influenced subsequent kanthas.

Modern Kumudini kantha with "folk" motifs

When the time came, however, to execute the kantha on cloth, Aarong hesitated. It was just about this time that Aarong, uptil now controlled by the Mennonite Church Council, was being handed over to BRAC. The women at the Jamalpur project had never made anything as ambitious as the newly designed kanthas. The finished kantha was to be so huge, that it would have to be made in sections and then put together afterwards. Wanting to be associated with the kantha revival, BRAC nevertheless was doubtful whether the revival could actually take place in Bangladesh itself. They were, however, willing to undertake the project, but with the work being done by Thai workers. The cost would, of course, be astronomical. It was at this point that Sister Michael Francis stepped in. Having worked with Bangladeshi women in jute works, she realized that they could be trained to embroider kanthas, which had, after all, been their traditional skill. She accordingly approached Kumudini with a proposal. If Kumudini was willing to cooperate with her, she could help train women to make kanthas. Kumudini had the organization, she had the energy and determination to reacquaint the Bangladeshi women with their traditional skill. Kumudini was willing and thus became the first, with Surayia Rahman's adaptation and Razia Qadir's design, to really initiate the kantha revival. Thus BRAC, which had spent several years training women in their kantha project at Jamalpur, was not there when the kantha was launched.

Training in kantha work at Kumudini involved teaching of mainly three stitches: the kantha stitch, the weave running stitch, and the Kashmiri stitch. The women were shown how the true kantha stitch was not a darning stitch. The stitches had to penetrate all the layers of the cloth, and they had to fall slightly ahead or behind the previous rows. It was only thus that the characteristic ripples of the kantha could be produced. The women were also taught to use the weave running stitch to create border patterns replicating the *par* patterns of sari borders.

At a kantha exhibition organized by BRAC/Shilpakala

But, apart from acquiring traditional kantha skills, the workers also learned a filling stitch to fill in large expanses of colour. In traditional kanthas, these large expanses of colour are filled by the typical kantha stitches: darning stitches, either minute pin-dot stitches or an interwoven darning stitch, *kaitya*, *chatai* or the kantha stitch. This process of working is slow, and, moreover, produces a muted effect. If the Kashmiri stitch is used instead, not only are the large expanses of colour filled in quickly, but the final result is also brighter. To distinguish between Kashmiri work and kantha work, Kumudini workers refer to embroidery using Kashmiri stitch as "tapestry" and embroidery using the kantha stitch in addition to Kashmiri stitch as *nakshi*. Workers also learned a fourth stitch: the stem or *dal*, which was used to outline motifs. Workers were taught finishing, how to begin and end neatly, clipping off loose threads.

Kumudini's greatest contribution, perhaps, has been in the kantha training it initiated. Initially started for the Sonargaon kanthas, the training programme has helped provide training in kantha work to women from several parts of Bangladesh. Batches of women, under the ILO training scheme, come to Kumudini for a month's training. They go back home subsequently, and help make kanthas and provide training to other women as well. Thus while Kumudini does not have branches as BRAC does in different *upazilas*, the women who go out after training have spread the influence of Kumudini to other parts of Bangladesh as well. Back in their own village they continue to do kantha work, supplementing the family income and continuing to produce kanthas and kantha embroidery.

Though BRAC could not be associated in the initial kantha breakthrough, it did not take long for it to catch up and become associated with the kantha in a big way. Realizing that the kantha could be made in Bangladesh once again, BRAC expanded the Jamalpur project to include more ambitious kanthas. The advantage that

BRAC had over Kumudini was that the workers lived near enough to be able to come to the centres and work there. At Kumudini work was always   taken home. Better organized and financially stronger than Kumudini, BRAC has—through its outlet Aarong—helped make kantha a household word. Able to provide facilities for its designers to visit Gurusaday Museum and Ashutosh Museum in Calcutta and get an exposure to kanthas, Aarong is encouraging the creation of new designs. Kumudini, on the other hand, appears to rely on its original fund of designs.

In March 1982, BRAC and Kumudini were joined by another NGO involved in kantha making. Surayia Rahman, who had been casually involved with Karika and Aarong, was approached by a Canadian, Maureen Berlin, with a proposal to set up a kantha centre. Surayia would work on the design and the embroidery; Maureen would work on marketing and at making the organization a women's development project. Initially an attempt was made to call the organization "Nakshi Kantha Kendra," but as the pieces planned were very definitely not kanthas proper—much as they had been influenced by kantha embroidery—the centre had to settle for the unwieldy name : Skill Development for Underprivileged Women. However, "Nakshi Kantha Kendra" was used as a sub-title, the Bengali "equivalent," and would later be the name of its marketing outlet. SDUW is an example of the changes taking place in the kantha, as well as an example of the role of kantha in women's development.

Like other organizations involved in handicrafts, SDUW is also devoted to women's development. However, while the other organizations are somewhat loosely organized, SDUW is highly organized in this regard. Thus while the women are trained in kantha making and embroidery, they also receive health care and family planning advice. Their children, if under three, are provided day care on the premises, if older are educated. Meals are provided to the children who accompany their mothers. However, to encourage family planning, care for more than two children is not given. The women are encouraged to be independent. Meals are not provided, but women can make a small contribution and a wholesome lunch is prepared with the money collected for the day. Women are taught hygiene and social skills. They are encouraged, rather expected, to bring a guardian when they first come, in order to encourage the development of the entire family and ensure domestic harmony.

At the same time, SDUW is an example of extreme commercialization and factory-type production. This does not, however, mean slipshod work, but the highly regulated work that we associate with factories as well as the division of labour that is a concomitant of mass production. It must be noted that SDUW work—especially that begun by Surayia Rahman—is sophisticated art and extreme care is taken to make the kanthas/ tapestries exquisite works of art. The process was designed with extreme care by Surayia Rahman—a process that she later adopted when she moved out from SDUW to her own organization, Arshi. Initially working with Surayia Rahman's designs, the SDUW had a repertoire of 80 designs. These designs were embroidered and kept in a display room so that future copies could be made on the basis of these designs. SDUW claims that only 250 editions of any one design would be made. At present, the number of designs has gone up, with the addition of other designers. However, SDUW seems to be relying mainly on the designs created by Surayia Rahman, and, very recently, on "rural" designs in books.

A brief description of the working of SDUW, initiated by Surayia Rahman—and continued at her new organization, Arshi—will give a fairly good idea of how different their work has become from traditional kantha work. Working from drawings, Surayia Rahman would make blueprints of the designs. These designs would then be traced onto the cloth. In order to ensure that there was no distortion in the lines, she would again go over the lines on the cloth. The design traced, it would then be given to the "thread girls" to sort out the coloured threads necessary for the embroidery.

The SDUW kanthas were made mainly for display as wall-hangings, so to ensure that there is no puckering of the cloth and no unevenness in the finished products, women use embroidery hoops. Working with the Kashmiri stitch, the women cover large areas of the cloth with close embroidery. The background of the tapestry is covered with close darning stitches, rather than the kantha stitch, thus eliminating the characteristic ripples of the kantha. This process continues at SDUW, though Surayia has since left.

The SDUW kanthas were planned with an eye on a foreign, sophisticated market, a market that had been prepared by the work of Aarong and Kumudini. Thus instead of cotton silk is used, and, in order to ensure perfection, trained girls embroider faces. These "face-girls" as they are called, work on the faces to achieve uniformly attractive and pleasant features. In order to ensure that they do not get thoroughly bored with their work, they are allowed to work on tapestries a few hours each day. From 8 in the morning to 3 in the afternoon they work on faces. Then from 3 to 5 they work on embroidery.

Once the tapestry is finished, it is washed. Then, while still damp, it is stretched and mounted on a wooden frame slightly larger than the tapestry. The tapestry is allowed to dry on the frame. The SDUW kanthas, therefore, have succeeded in eliminating uneven kanthas and "ugly" human features that often ruin kanthas. Some very fine pieces have been executed at SDUW, but the astronomical prices of the SDUW tapestries restrict purchases to foreigners and those few Bangladeshis whose incomes bear no relation to the Bangladeshi average. A tapestry based on Jasimuddin's *Sojan Badiyar Ghat*, for instance, costs Taka 28,000.

SDUW has perhaps effected the greatest change in kantha embroidery, both in stitchcraft and themes. Surayia

Kumudini wall-hanging

Aarong cushion cover

Sojan Badiyar Ghat: Wall-hanging designed by Surayia Rahman

A drawing room decorated with cushions in kantha embroidery

A bedroom with kantha work furnishings

Kantha designed by Razia Qadir

Rahman introduced themes based on folk tales, legends, narrative and dramatic poems. Just as Jasimuddin had been inspired by the work of Bengali women to write about the embroidered quilt, so too did Surayia Rahman, inspired by Jasimuddin's poem, try to make kanthas that told stories as Shaju's kantha did. In his poem, Jasimuddin imaginatively recreated an embroidered quilt into which a Bengali woman might weave the joys and sorrows of her life, and Surayia in turn embroidered the poet's vision in an embroidered quilt. One art influenced the other, and then was again influenced by it. Surayia's contribution is therefore to the kanthas that display vignettes of life of rural Bengal, capturing in needle and thread a way of life that is fast disappearing. At the same, time, Surayia is aware of the nostalgia for a Mughal and colonial past. Thus, she has designed Mughal scenes and scenes depicting the British Raj.

While one might not agree with Surayia Rahman's use of Mughal scenes for kantha work, or her interpolating non-folk elements into kantha embroidery, there is no doubt that Surayia Rahman is an artist. The typical Surayia Rahman tapestry is packed with stuff similar to the traditional kantha. Furthermore, there is a creative impulse in her work, which does not merely replicate old kanthas. Though she transformed old kanthas into the popular *Sonargaon* design, she did not copy the design blindly. For instance, the gentleman smoking a *hookah* is not ensconced in his chair, he seems to be rising from it. The design has been copied countless times since Surayia first drew it, but Surayia explains why there is a gap between the gentleman and the chair : "He is rising from his chair in ecstasy at the dancers."

Critics of SDUW are quick to point out that, lovely as the tapestries are, they are not true kanthas. Nevertheless, drawing on the kantha tradition, the SDUW tapestries have attracted people who have not been quite won over by the Aarong and Kumudini muted work. Working with folk scenes, idealized rural scenes, as well with folk tales and Jasimuddin's narrative poems, SDUW has created colourful, bright kanthas. These colourful, bright kanthas have influenced Aarong and Kumudini as well.

In 1988, following a dispute over copyright, Surayia Rahman left SDUW and started her own organization, Arshi. The story behind her break with SDUW suggests the great difference between the commercial kantha and the earlier traditional one. There were no copyrights on traditional motifs and designs. Kantha makers borrowed freely, imitating closely where they would, deviating when they wished.

Each Surayia Rahman piece, however, is stamped unmistakably hers. The individual hand in traditional kanthas, on the other hand, is revealed in the exquisiteness of embroidery. More to the purpose, therefore, is work such as exemplified by women like Latifa Begum of Chilmari who "design" and execute kanthas. Latifa Begum's example, nevertheless, suggests that it is still necessary to guide the kantha maker.

Since the early 80s, Sayyada R. Ghuznavi had been working with a small group of women and young girls in Chilmari and Kurigram in an effort to revive kanthas typical to the region. Latifa Begum and others of the group were shown a selection of photographs and a few examples of old kanthas. Based on these, the women executed one-of-a kind kanthas. Since 1983 limited editions of kanthas have been produced by the group, exclusively in natural dyed yarn. They are commissioned and marketed by Aranya at home and abroad. Broad outlines and layouts are prepared in advance, with the craftswomen having the liberty to select the border designs, additional motifs and the combination of stitches and colours adding to the beauty of each kantha. One of these pieces won Latifa Begum the National Award for Master Craftsman in 1984.

From its quiet beginning in 1974, the kantha has emerged as one of the living crafts of Bangladesh. There has been change and adaptation; old designs have been arranged in new ways; contemporary scenes have been embroidered in traditional stitches. There have been good and bad kanthas; much work has been of poor quality. But in this profusion of kanthas, one or two really excellent pieces have emerged that would never have been possible without this revival.

Perhaps what is most important is that the revival of an almost lost art has provided several thousand women with a livelihood. Also, as most organizations have literacy, savings, health projects—though perhaps not all as regimented as SDUW—these women have benefited in manifold ways. Moreover, inability to purchase really exquisite pieces has a positive side to it. At the BRAC/Shilpakala Nakshi Kantha exhibition in April, 1992, several earnest young women—not associated with any handicrafts organization—were busily copying down borders and motifs, and learning how to embroider kantha fashion from the kantha makers exhibiting their kantha-making skills. Like the kantha makers of old, these women were learning how to make kanthas for love, not money.

It is also necessary at this point to talk about the kantha revival in West Bengal. It should be remembered that India is richer in kantha collections than Bangladesh—though almost all the kanthas were collected from the area which is now Bangladesh. The revival of this traditional Bengal art took place in West Bengal at about the same time as in Bangladesh. The "ethnic" look had become popular. Moreover, the influx of refugees from Bangladesh during the 1971 war also encouraged the development of a craft known to them.

The kantha revival in West Bengal was, however, more geared to dress fashions. Thus kantha embroidery was used to embellish saris, *kameezes* and shawls. While the kantha revival in Bangladesh attempted consciously to revive a traditional craft and then use it for contemporary purposes, in West Bengal the kantha revival was initially more commercialized. Thus "attractive" designs were sought, designs which would catch the eye and sell. The common designs—labelled "Shantiniketan" because of the work produced in this area—tended to be floral, more akin to the arabesques of Rajshahi *sujni* embroidery than to traditional kantha motifs. Colours used for the embroidery were bright, almost veering on the loud and gaudy. To enable quicker production, thicker strands of thread were used. Stitches too tended to be larger. Background stitching was absent. The rapidity of execution led to a reduction in costs. Thus, one may buy a *tussore* sari worked in kantha embroidery for Rs. 1500, whereas at SDUW the embroidery alone on a sari might cost Taka 3000.

Another feature of West Bengal work is the "Indianization" of the designs, rather than a conscious re-creation of traditional Bengal motifs. In early Bengal kanthas, the women may be seen in various costumes. Some, for instance, appear to be dressed in *choli* and *ghagra*. However, the female figures in these old kanthas still seem to belong to the Bengal countryside. On the other hand, the new West Bengal kanthas have designs where in feature and in dress women appear Rajasthani. The Bengal kantha artist usually drew her faces frontally, but many West Bengal kantha artists, perhaps in imitation of the *chamba rumals*, are drawing profiles. The god Ganesh is also making his appearance—not very surprising as much of the kantha revival, as Ashish Chakraborty, Curator of the Gurusaday Museum, points out, has been at the initiative of the Marwari business community. Similarly in Bangladesh, socio-cultural factors are also distinguishing new kanthas from traditional ones. There is thus, in several new kanthas, an "Islamization," which often leads to the attempt to claim a Mughal heritage. It is not Surayia Rahman alone who is designing Mughal scenes for kanthas.

Because of the tendency of folk art to absorb different influences, and because the kantha revival was made with an eye on the market, it is not surprising that the kantha revival in Bangladesh and West Bengal should show these divergences. West Bengal is, after all, a part of India; Bangladesh is a separate nation attempting to establish a separate cultural identity.

However, while much of the kantha work in West Bengal is strictly and unabashedly commercial, there are a number of organizations which are trying to revive the old tradition. Thus the kanthas produced at the kantha centres of the Crafts Council of West Bengal attempt to replicate in design and stitchcraft the old kanthas preserved in museums. What is very remarkable is that they have attempted to avoid the Kashmiri stitch—unlike Bangladeshi kantha makers—and are using the running stitch even for filling motifs. Apart from the interwoven darning stitch, they are also reproducing the ribbed running stitch and the diminutive running stitch. Thus along with the variegated designs and textures created by the kantha stitch and the *kaitya* and *chatai*, the Crafts Council kanthas have ribbed areas interspersed with minuscule dots.

In both Bangladesh and West Bengal today may be seen the conscious attempt to revive a lost craft, as well as the temptation for complacency and rapid production of popular designs. At the same time there is an endeavour to recreate a lost tradition where art and craft blend into one indistinguishable whole.

Kantha Collections[1]

Bangladesh

Public Collections :
Bangla Academy
Design Centre, BSCIC
Folk Art and Crafts Foundation, Sonargaon.
Bangladesh National Museum

Private Collections :
Sayyada R. Ghuznavi
Hameeda Hossain
Mohammed Sayeedur
Tofail Ahmed
Jahanara Abedin (The Zainul Abedin Collection)

India

Ashutosh Museum, Calcutta
Calico Museum of Textiles, Ahmedabad
Gurusaday Museum, Thakurpukur
Indian Museum

France

Association pour 1 'Etude et la Documentation des Textiles
d' Aise

Japan

Hiroko Iwatate Collection

---

1. Some of this information is drawn from *Woven Air*

United Kingdom
British Library (India Office Library and Records)
Leicestershire Museums
National Museums of Scotland
Victoria and Albert Museum

United States of America
Philadelphia Museum of Art
The Smithsonian Institution, Washington D.C.
The Textile Museum, Washington D. C.

Craft Organizations Which Make Kanthas
Bangladesh Rural Advancement Committee (BRAC), outlet Aarong
Kumudini Welfare Trust
Karika
Banchte Shekha, Jessore
Friends of Bangladesh, Tongi
Bangladesh Small and Cottage Industries Corporation (BSCIC)
Aranya

Organizations which have been influenced by kanthas but make tapestry that is not strictly kantha are the following :
Arshi
Skill Development for Underprivileged Women/Nakshi Kantha Kendra
Jamnakshi

Bibliography

Abedin, Zainul."Amader Shilpakala" (Our Arts and Crafts). *Mashik Mohammadi, Ashar* 1365 (September 1958).

Agrawala, V. S. "Kalpavriska: The Wish Fulfilling Tree." *Journal of the Indian Society of Oriental Art,* Vol. 1, 1934.

Ahmed, Sayeed. "Bangladesh Handicrafts." *Bangladesh Handicrafts 1974* (Catalogue of Bangladesh Handicraft Exhibition). Dacca: Bangladesh Handicraft Show Committee [1974], 4-5.

Ahmed, Perveen. "Kantha—The Embroidered Quilt." Unpublished article.

Ahmed, Tofail. *Amader Prachin Shilpa* (Our Ancient Crafts). Dhaka: Naoroz Kitabistan, 1964.

_____. *Lokshilpa* (Folk Art) Dhaka: Bangla Academy, 1985.

_____. "Nakshi Kantha." *Shilpakala,* January 1992: 60-72.

_____, Shafiqul Ameen, Abdul Matin Sarkar and Muhammad Saidur. "Popular Art in Bangladesh" *Culture* (UNESCO), Vol. VIII, 1981: 121-141.

_____, Hameeda Hossain and Mohammad Sayeedur. "Survey of Folk Crafts and Documentation of Designs in Bangladesh: A Narrative Report." Dhaka: Bangladesh Hastashilpa Samabaya Federation (Karika), 1988. Mimeo.

Ahmed, Wakil. *Banglar Lok Sanskriti* (Folk Culture of Bengal). Dhaka, 1974.

Alam, Syed Mahbub. "Lok Shilper Jatitattik Bishleshon O Mullayon: Proshongo Nakshi Kantha." *Bangladesher Lok Shilpa,* Dhaka, 1983: 146-154.

Aryan, B. N. "A Rich Folk Expression." *Swagat* (In-flight Magazine of Indian Airlines), Oct. 1992: 23-27.

Banerjee, N.N. *Monograph on The Cotton Fabrics of Bengal.* Calcutta, 1898.

Bangladesh Handicrafts 1974. Dacca: Bangladesh Handicraft Show Committee [1974].

Bhattacharjee, Surovi. "The Weaver's Art of Bengal." *The Costumes and Textiles of India*. Ed. J.B. Bhusan. Bombay, 1956.

Bhavnani, Enakshi. *Decorative Designs and Craftsmanship of India*. Bombay, 1974.

Bhusan, J. B. *The Costumes and Textiles of India*. Bombay, 1956.

Bonaventura, Paul and Beth Stockley. *Woven Air: The Muslin and Kantha Tradition of Bangladesh*. London, 1988.

Chakraborty, Ashish. Personal communication. February 24, 1993.

Chatterjee, Tapan Mohan. *Alpona*. Calcutta, 1965.

Chattopadhyay, Kamaladevi. *Carpets and Floor Coverings of India*. Bombay, 1969.

_____. *Handicrafts of India*. New Delhi, 1975.

_____. *Indian Embroidery*. New Delhi, 1977.

Chaudhuri, Nirad. C. *The Autobiography of an Unknown Indian*. New York , 1951.

Chen, Martha Alter. "Kantha and Jamdani Revival in Bangladesh." *Indian International Centre Quarterly*, Vol. 2:4 (Dec. 1984).

Christensen, E.O. *Primitive Art*. New York, 1955.

Coomaraswamy, A. K. *Introduction to Indian Art*. Delhi, 1965.

Das, Abinas Chandra. *Rgvedic Culture,* Calcutta, 1925.

Dutt, G. S. "The Art of Kantha," *Modern Review*, Calcutta, 1939.

5000 Indian Designs and Motifs. The Indian Institute of Art in Industry, Calcutta, 1965.

Fokker, N. *Persian and Other Oriental Carpets for Today*. London, 1973.

Ganguly, Kalyan Kumar. *Design in Traditional Arts of Bengal*. Calcutta, 1973.

Ghuznavi, Sayyada R. *Naksha: A Collection of Designs of Bangladesh*. Dhaka, 1981.

Gupta, G. N. *The Industries and Resources of Eastern Bengal and Assam for 1907-1908*. Shillong, 1908.

Hauser, A. *The Social History of Art*, Vol. 1. Translated Stanley Godman. London, 1952.

Karika: Bangladesh Hastashilpa Samabaya Federation Ltd. "A Study of the Activities and Organizational Aspects." October, 1986. Mimeo.

Hafiz, Abdul. "Embroideries of Bangladesh." *An Anthology of Crafts of Bangladesh.* Dhaka, 1987.

Hossain, Hameeda. "Organising Women's Employment Through Kantha Production." *Woven Air: The Kantha and Muslin Tradition of Bangladesh.* Ed. Paul Bonaventura and Beth Stockley. London, 1988. p. 57-58.

_ ___. "Symbolism and Tradition of the Nakshi Kantha (Embroidered Quilt)." Paper read at Seminar organized by Folk Art and Crafts Foundation, February 1983.

_____. Personal interview. May 18, 1992.

_____. Tofail Ahmed, and Mohammad Sayeedur. "Survey of Folk Crafts and Documentation of Designs in Bangladesh: A Narrative Report. " Dhaka, 1988. Mimeo.

_____. *Nakshamala: Nakshi Kantha.* Dhaka, 1987.

Hunter, W. W. *The Annals of Rural Bengal.* London, 1868.

Islam, Nazrul. *Shreshta Kabita.* Dhaka, 1974.

Iyer, Bharata K. *Indian Art: A Short Introduction.* Bombay, 1958.

Jasimuddin. *Nakshi Kanthar Maath.* Calcutta, 1929.

_____. *The Field of the Embroidered Quilt.* 1939. Trans. E.M. Milford. Revised W. Mc Dermott. Dhaka, 1964.

_____. "Purba Banglar Nakshi Kantha O Sari." 1958. Reprinted in *Bangladesher Lok Oitijja.* Ed. Shamsuzzaman Khan. Dhaka, 1985. 268-274.

Kramrisch, Stella. "Kantha." *Journal of the Indian Society of Oriental Art,* Vol. 7 (1939). 141-167.

_____. *Unknown India: Ritual Art in Tribe andVillage.* Philadelphia, 1968.

Liley, Alison. *The Craft of Embroidery.* London, 1961.

Majid, Fahmida. "Alpana." Notes written for the Commonwelth Institute. London, November 1983.

Maury, Curt. *Folk Origins of Indian Art.* New York, 1969.

Mehta, R. J. *The Handicrafts and Industrial Arts of India.* Bombay, 1960.

Mode, Heinz and Subodh Chandra. *Indian Folk Art.* Tr. from the German by Peter & Betty Ross. Bombay, 1985.

Mookerjee, Ajit. *Folk Art of Bengal.* Calcutta, 1939.

Mukerjee, Radhakamal. *The Flowering of Indian Art.* Bombay, 1968.

Mukharji, T. N. *Art Manufactures of India* (Specially Compiled for the Glass-International Exhibition, 1888) Calcutta, 1888. Reprint New Delhi, 1974.

Pope, A.U. *Persian Architecture*. New York, 1965.

Radhakrishnan. *Principal Upanishads*. London, 1953.

Rahman, Mukhlesur. "Banglar Lokshilpa: Nakshi Kantha." *Varendra Shahitya Parishad Patrika*, 1367, B. S.

Sayeedur, Mohammad. "Loukik Chitrakalar Alpana" (Folk Art in the Alpana). *Purba Banglar Lok Sanskriti* (Folk Culture of East Bengal). Ed. Dular Choudhury, Calcutta.

_____. "The Common Ground." *Woven Air*. 23-27.

_____. "Symbols and Rituals in the Art of the Nakshi Kantha." *Woven Air*. 29-31.

_____. Personal interviews at various times.

Sen, Dinesh Chandra. *Brihat Banga*. Calcutta, 1935.

Vedantatirtha, Girish Chandra. *Prachin Shilpa Parichaya* (Introduction to Ancient Arts and Crafts). Calcutta, [1942].

Zaman, Niaz. "Nakshi Kantha." *The Bangladesh Observer*, June 19, 1977.

_____. "Kanthas of Bangladesh," *Shilpakala*, Vol. II (1979). 64-70.

_____. "Embroidered Quilt: A Living Art Form." *The Bangladesh Times*, August, 1980.

_____. *Animal Tales From Bangladesh*. Dhaka, 1985.

_____. "New Kanthas from Old." *Holiday*, April 24.

_____. *Lalitkala* (Journal of the Bangladesh National Museum), Vol. 2:1, Jan-June 1993.

Glossary

Aatchala : with eight triangles or segments; term derived from *aatchala*, meaning eight-roofed. *Chala* refers to the sloping roofs of huts. Thus roofs can be *dochala*, with two segments, or *charchala* having four segments.

Addhi : fine white cloth.

Almirah : closet.

Alpana : ritual drawings painted on the floor with a paste of ground rice flour.

Anaj taga : lit. vegetable border; a border pattern resembling a row of beans.

Anarasi : resembling a pineapple; name of a pattern worked with the Holbein stitch; known as *lik phul* at Rajshahi.

Anna : food; sustenance.

Apas : peace.

Arshi : mirror.

Arshilata : wrap for mirror.

Ashon : seat.

Astadal padma : eight-petalled lotus.

Bakhya : the back stitch.

Balish kantha : a pillow cover.

Balisher chapa, oshar : a pillow cover.

Barfi : diamond shaped motif.

Barochala : with twelve triangles, or segments; see *aatchala*.

Bashon dhakar rumal : a cover for plates.

Batua : bag; purse.

Beki   : wavy.

Beri   : a pair of curved tongs meant for pots.

Bhaduli Brata Alpana : an *alpana* drawn during the *Bhaduli Brata*, a prayer for the well-being of father, husband, son.

Bhorat phor : filling stitch.

Bichche par : the scorpion border.

Bisa taga   : the waist garland border; a *bisa* or *bicha* is a jewelled girdle.

Bostani   : a square wrapper for books.

Bothi   : a fish cutter; it is held in place on the floor with the soles of the feet, leaving both hands free to manipulate the item being cut.

Buddhu Bhutum : the name of a folk tale.

Chaka or *chakra* : wheel.

Charchala   : with four triangles or segments; see *aatchala*.

Chatai   : woven matting; the name of a stitch resembling matting ; also known as *pati phor*.

Chik taga   : the name of a border; literally the necklet border.

Chok par   : the eye border.

Dastarkhan : a spread for an eating place.

Devata   : deity.

Dhaner shish : paddy stalk.

Dheki   : rice husker.

Dhoti   : white lower garment worn by Hindu males, also as a sari by widows.

Dukkhu   : the unfortunate.

Durba   : a kind of grass.

Gach   : tree.

Gadla   : roughly stitched quilt.

Gatri   : wrapper for books or other valuables; also known as *bostani* and *bayton*.

Ghat   : the bank of a pond or river.

Gilaf   : envelope-shaped wrap for the Quran.

Golok dhanda : maze; the name of a motif; also known as *muchri* and *shostir chinho*.

Gopis   : village maidens; cow girls.

Grafi taga : the name of a border.

Guna	:	quality.
Gut	:	the name of a border.
Hulud	:	turmeric; also ceremony before marriage consisting of application of ground raw turmeric all over the body followed by a ritual bath.
Jainamaz	:	Muslim prayer mat.
Jati	:	betel cutter.
Jhop taga	:	name of border design; literally, the bush border.
Kaitya	:	bending; the name of a stitch which appears to slope.
Kajal	:	lamp black used as cosmetic; also to mark a dot on a child's forehead for warding off the evil eye.
Kalam	:	pen.
Kalka	:	paisley pattern.
Kalpavrksa	:	the wish-fullfilling tree.
Kanha	:	outer borders of a sujni.
Kapa	:	two pieces of cloth measuring about 4′ by 6′ worn by Muslim women of Chapai Nawabganj. One piece is worn as a *lungi*, the other is draped over the top.
Kautar khupi	:	pigeon coops; the name of a motif.
Khat kantha	:	kantha meant for use in a palanquin.
Khejur chhori	:	date branch.
Khol	:	cover.
Kula	:	winnowing fan.
Lagan	:	also called the *hulud*. One of the rituals is the tying of a *rakhi* or string round the wrist signifying the marital union.
Lep kantha	:	thickly quilted kantha, meant for use in winter.
Lik	:	Holbein stitch; patterns made using this stitch.
Lik jhumka	:	*lik* pattern resembling *jhumka* or earrings.
Lik lohori	:	*lik* pattern resembling waves.
Lik phor	:	the Holbein stitch.
Lik phul	:	*lik* pattern resembling a flower; known also as *shaita phul* in Rajshahi, *anarasi* in Jessore.
Lik tan	:	an elongated version of the *lik* pattern.
Lik tile	:	*lik* pattern resembling roofing tiles.
Lohira	:	wavy; see *Lohori*.
Loria	:	variation of *lohira*; see *Lohori*.

Lohori	:	mutation of Persian *"lehr"*; same as *lohira* and *loria*; name of kantha with a wave motif; but also applies to other kanthas using the thick, close running stitch associated with this type of kantha.
Lungi	:	sarong-type garment tucked round body to hang from waist to ankle.
Maach taga	:	the fish border.
Makara	:	fish-crocodile figure associated with Hindu religious art.
Mala taga	:	the garland border.
Mama	:	maternal uncle.
Mangal Charaner Alpana	:	*alpana* drawn when a marriage is fixed.
Moi taga	:	ladder border.
Motor dana	:	pea border.
Muchri	:	same as *golok dhanda* and *shostir chinho*.
Nakshi Kanthar Maath	:	the field of the embroidered quilt; the name of a poem by Jasimuddin.
Nakshi pitha	:	rice-flour cake made with elaborate designs.
Nolok taga	:	nose ring border.
Oar	:	pillow cover.
Palkir topor	:	palanquin cloth.
Panch mala taga	:	literally, the five-garland border; same as *panch taga*.
Panch taga	:	a threaded running stitch border.
Panchomul	:	literally five-rooted; a five-pronged motif common in Rajshahi *sujnis*.
Panja	:	the open palm; symbol among the Shias of the holy pentad, comprising the Prophet Mohammad, Hazrat Ali, Fatima, the Prophet's daughter and Ali's wife, and Hazrat Imam Hasan and Hazrat Imam Hussain, the children of Ali and Fatima and the Prophet's grandsons.
Par tola	:	embroidered with sari border patterns.
Pati phor	:	also known as *chatai*; lit. the mat stitch.
Phor	:	stitch.
Phulkari	:	a form of embroidery common to the Punjab, worked with patterned running stitches.
Phul par	:	flower border.
Pipal	:	the banyan tree.
Pipre sari	:	the name of a border pattern based on the *kaitya*, literally, ant line.

Pirs	:	popular saints.
Pocha	:	rotten.
Puja	:	Hindu religious ceremony.
Puranaghata	:	the full vase.
Rajas	:	passion.
Rath	:	carriage with wheels carrying images of Vishnu.
Rens taga	:	a threaded stitch border resembling a pattern of wrenches.
Rumal	:	handkerchief.
Sagar	:	sea.
Salu	:	red material used for cotton padded quilt; also for *sujni* and cross stitch kanthas.
Sarir par	:	sari border.
Satadal	:	hundred-petalled.
Satadal padma	:	the hundred-petalled lotus.
Sattva	:	purity, truth.
Shaita phul	:	also known as *lik phul* and *anarast*.
Shamuk taga	:	the snail border.
Sharia	:	Islamic code of laws.
Shoja	:	straight.
Shostir chinho	:	the swastika, also known as *muchri* or *golok dhanda*.
Sijda	:	touching the forehead to the ground in Muslim prayer.
Sujni	:	in Bihar, quilts similar to Bengal kanthas; in Bangladesh specifically quilts made with red *salu*, worked with back stitch.
Surma dani	:	container for antimony oxide, used as eye cosmetic.
Ta'abiz par	:	amulet border; name of border pattern resembling an amulet design.
Taika	:	spindle.
Tamas	:	darkness.
Tejas	:	heat; fire.
Triratna	:	three jewels.
Uzu	:	ritual ablutions preceding Muslim prayer.

Index

A

Aarong, 5,7,25-6, 138, 141-2,
   148, 153-4
Aatchala, 111, 126
Abedin, Jahanara, 159
Abedin, Zainul, 3, 139-40, 159
Addhi, 23, 116
Aeroplane, 74
Agrawala, V. S., 74
Agricultural implements, 64,
   90
Ahmed, Perveen, 15, 146
Ahmed, Sayeed, 127
Ahmed, Tofail, 3, 16, 17, 106,
   115, 125, 141, 159
Alpana, 2, 25, 41-3, 70, 73, 80,
   84, 89
Anaj taga, 95, 103
Anarasi, kantha, 111; stitch, 52
Animal motifs, 90
Aranya, 154, 160
Arrowhead, 57, 94
Arshi, 5, 147, 160
Arshilata, 6, 13, 62
Ashon, 6, 13, 61, 63, 108
Ashutosh Museum, 146, 159
Asoka, 74
Astadal padma, 76

B

Backstitch, 6, 58
Background stitching, 6,31-2,
   51

Bakhya, 58
Balish kantha, 62
Balisher chapa, see *Balish*
   kantha
Balisher oshar, 6, 13, 62
Banerjee, N. N., 106
Bangla Academy,139, 159
Bangladesh Small and
   Cottage Industries
   Corporation, BSCIC, 139,
   159, 160
Bangladesh National
   Museum, 111, 159
Bangladesh Rural Advance-
   ment Committee, BRAC,
   5,7,24, 123, 141-3, 145-6, 160
Bankura, 106
Barfi, 96
Barisal kantha, 137
Barochala, 111, 126
Bashon dhakar rumal, 63
Batua, 33
Bayton, 32, 61
Beki, 63, 83, 96
Belayeti sujni, 116
Beri, 71, 92
Betel cutter, 72, 92
Betel leaf, 134
Bhaduli brata alpana, 4
Bhatacharjee, Surovi, 50
Bhorat phor, 57, 123; see
   Kashmiri stitch
Bicche par, 50,95
Bicycle, 73
Birds, 71,73,135

Birdwood, George, 13,14
Bisa taga, 103
Boat, 84,137
Bogra, 135
Borders, 94-107
Bostani, 32,61,134
Bothi, 92
Brahmanic, 71
Brata, 41-3
Brihat Banga ,17
British influence, 114
Buddha, 89
Buddhist art, 71, 89
Buddhu Bhutum, 15
Buttonhole stitch, 58, 127
Brikshalata, 6

C

Carpet kantha, 5, 23, 24, 30, 114-5
Central lotus, 108, 109, 134
Central motif, 31, 64
Chain stitch, 127
Chakra, 48, 79
Chakraborty, Ashish, 156
Chamba rumals, 156
Chandra, Subodh, 64
Chapai Nawabganj Mahila Sangstha, 114
Charchala, 111, 126
Chatterjee, Tapan Mohan, 41, 72
Chatai, 31, 47-9, 50, 82, 125, 127, 137, 138, 157
Chattopadhyaya, Kamaladevi, 13, 19, 80
Chaudhuri, Nirad C., 25
Chik taga, 103
Children's kanthas, 62
Chilmari, 125, 154
Chok par, 96; *taga* 103
Chhop tana, 111
Colour, of kanthas, 24-6, 126-7,138
Comb, 72, 92
Coomarasawmy, A. K., 71, 74
Corner motif, 31, 64, 69

Crafts Council of West Bengal, 59, 157
Crescent, 79
Cross stitch, 58; kantha, 108, 125

D

Dal phor, 57, 145; see stem stitch
Darius, palace of, 28, 74
Darning stitch, 7, 31-2, 44, 51, 127, 138, 148
Dastarkhan, 6, 9, 39, 62, 63
Deer, 5
Design Centre, 3
Dhaka, 106
Dhaner shish, 5, 95
Dheki, 72
Dhoti, 1, 8, 22
Diamond, 73, 109
Duldul, 90
Durga, 37
Durjani , 62
Dutt, G.S.,17, 50-1, 60,94, 106

E

Earring, 72, 92
Earth, 70, 75
East Pakistan Small and Cottage Industries Corporation, 3, 139-40
Elephant, 5,6,76, 90, 134
Evil eye, 36
European design, 14

F

Fairy, 38
Fairy tale, 14, 15
Faridpur, 3, 39, 94
Faridpur kanthas, 39, 58, 108, 110, 126-34
Feather stitch, 94
Fish cutter, 72

Fish, 70, 71, 73, 84, 137
Floral motifs, 5,37,64, 137
Flowers, 73
Folk art, 8, 135, 156-7
Folk Art and Crafts
    Foundation, 3, 139, 159
Folk, belief, 36-7, 40, 94;
    lore, 14; magic, 40-1;
    scenes, 153; tales, 153
Footprint, 89

G

Gach, 122
Gadla, 61
Geometrical motifs, 73
Ghar hashia, 52
Ghuznavi, Sayyada R., 42,154,
    159
Gilaf, 6, 33, 39, 62
Golok dhanda, 80
Gopichandra, Raja, 14, 16
Gopis, 39, 109
Grafi taga, 95, 106
Great Mountain, 83
Gujrati stitch, 58
Gurusaday Museum, 43, 107,
    146, 156
Gut taga, 103

H

Hasan, Qamrul, 3, 139
Herringbone stitch, 57, 127
Hindu, iconography, 37-9, 74;
    influences, 37-9;
    mythology, 37, 74
Holbein stitch, 52
Hooghly, 106
Hossain, Hameeda, 106, 140,
    141, 159
Horse, 90, 135
Human figures, 64
Hundred-petalled lotus, 70,
    76
Hunting scene, 90
Hurricane lamp, 73

I

Indian Museum, 159
Indus Valley, 69, 80
Islam, Nazrul, 15
Iyer, Bharata, 71

J

Jagannath, 38, 89
Jainamaz, 39, 61
Jamalpur, 7, 38, 125, 135, 145
Jamalpur kanthas, 83, 135
Jasimuddin, 16-21, 36, 61, 124,
    148, 153
Jati, 92
Jessore, 3, 7, 49, 94, 106, 125
Jessore-Faridpur kanthas, 126-
    134
Jessore, kanthas, 70, 83, 110,
    111, 126-7, 134; stitch, 51-2,
    127
Jhop taga, 95

K

Kaitya, 31, 49-50, 77, 79-80
Kajal lata, 72, 127, 137, 138,
    145, 157
Kalam, 106
Kalka, 48, 57, 64, 82, 127, 134
Kalpavrksa, 71
Kantha, motif, 92; phor,
    see Kantha stitch; stitch, 7,
    31-2, 134, 138, 143, 145
Kapa, 22, 27, 110
Kapasia, 125
Karika, 5, 141, 160
Kashmiri bhorat, 52, 57; also
    see Kashmiri stitch; shawls,
    57, 70, 82; stitch, 82, 123,
    138, 143, 145
Kautar khupi, 83, 110, 111
Khat kantha, 58
Khejur chhori, 92
Khulna kanthas, 134-5

Kitchen implements, 71, 72, 92

Kramrisch, Stella, 17, 24, 36, 42, 44-7, 51, 59, 60, 61,70

Krishna, 37, 39, 108

Kula, 70, 72, 83, 92; see also Kitchen implements

Kumudini, 7, 24, 26, 138, 143, 145-6

Kurigram, 154

Kushtia, 3, 94, 125, 128, 135

Kushtia-Bogra kanthas, 137

Kushtia stitch, 50

L

Lakshmi, 37, 75, 89

Lakshmi's footprints, 38, 73, 89

Leaf, 64, 80

Lep kantha, 61

Lik, jhumka, 112; kantha, 33, 108, 111, 122, 123; *lohori,* 111; *phor,* see *Lik* stitch; stitch 52, 126; *phul,* 111; *tan,* 112; tile, 112

Lohira, see *Lohori*

Lohori, kantha, 23, 24, 27, 32-3, 108, 109-111, 125, 137; motif, 23, 49, 81, 83, 84; stitch, 46;

Loria, see *Lohori*

Lotus, 20, 64, 69, 70,74-9; central, 64, 70

Lungi, 1,8,22,23

M

Muslim influences, 34-6, 37-40

Maach, par 103; *taga,* 95

Magic, see folk magic

Makara, 84

Mala taga, 102

Manada Sundari, 43, 60, 104, 107

Manipuri quilt, 124

Maury, Curt, 75

Mayur pankhi, 84

Mauryan art, 71

Megasthenes, 13

Meghna, 124

Mehta, R. J., 44

Mode, Heinz, 64

Mohenjodaro, 80

Moi taga, 102

Monkey, 83

Mookerjee, Ajit, 17, 73

Moon, 79

Mosque, 89

Motor dana, 95, 96,

Mountain, 83; Great Mountain, 83

Muchri, 80

Mukherjee, Radhakamal, 80

Mymensingh kanthas, 58, 127, 135

Mymensingh-Jamalpur kanthas, 135

Myths, 64

N

Nadia, 106

Nakshamala, 141

Nakshi, 16, 108, 145

Nakshi kantha, 16, 17, 23, 61, 108, 127, 134, 137; *Nakshi Kantha* ,141

Nakshi Kantha Kendra, 146

Nakshi Kanthar Maath, 3, 16, 17-21, 124

Nakshi pitha, 141

National Handicrafts Exhibition, 140-1

Nolok taga, 103

O

Oar, 59, 62

P

Pabna, 106, 135

Palanquin, 72,73,74, 92

Palkir topor, 61
Palm, 89
Panch taga,panch mala taga, 102
Panchomul, 122
Panja, 89
Par tola kantha, 106, 108-9,
    127, 134, 135
Parrot, 74
Pati phor, 47, 125, 138
Pattern darning, 47-9
Peacock, 5, 90, 127, 134
Peacock-prowed boat, 84
Persian, influence, 115, 116;
    motifs, 74
Phul ,kantha, 61-3;*par*, 95
Phulkari, 48-9
Pipal, 82
Pipre sari, 47, 92
Portuguese, 13

R

Radha, 37, 108
Radhakrishnan, 25
Rags, 36, 62
Rahman, Surayia, 20-1, 146,
    147-8, 153-4
Rahman, Mohammad
    Sayeedur, see Sayeedur,
    Mohammad
Raja Rampur, 116
Rajshahi, 3, 22, 24, 27, 37, 49,
    58, 125-6; kanthas, 22, 49,
    58, 70, 111, 125-6, 134;
    sujnis, 115-22
Rangpur, 22, 135
Rath, 38, 89, 134
Religion, influence on kantha,
    37-9
Rens taga, 106
Rumal, 63
Running stitch, 44-7
Running stitch kantha 108-111
Rural scenes, 142
Rgveda, 13

S

Salu, 5, 23, 111,116
Sagar taga, 83, 103
Santals, 73,83
Sari, 1,6,8,22,27,36, 124
Sarir par kantha, 109; see also
    Par tola kantha
Satadal padma, 70,76
Satin stitch, 58
Sayeedur, Mohammad, 14, 27,
    41,63, 138,139,141,159
Sen, Dinesh Chandra, 17, 124
Sirajuddin, Mohammad, 90
Sister Michael Francis, 142-3
Skill Development for Under-
    privileged Women, SDUW,
    5,7,20,23, 32,33, 138, 146-8,
    153-4, 160
Sojan Badiyar Ghat, 148
Superstition, 8, 94
Svastika, 71
Swastika, 73,80
Sylhet, 17, 124
Symbolic motifs, 70, 71
Sonargaon Hotel, 1,2,4,123
Star, 77
Stem stitch, 57,145
Sujni, 23, 5, 22, 30, 37, 60,
    115-22,125, 126, 153, 156
Sujni kantha, 60, 61
Sun, 70,76,79
Surmadani, 92,134

T

Taabiz par, 95,102
Tagore, Abindranath, 17, 20,
    124
Taika, 32
Tantric, 73
Tapestry, 123
Textile pattern kanthas, 50
Thread, 4, 24-6, 32
Threaded running stitch,
    52,102
Tiger, 90, 134

Tin phor 58; also see Cross
    stitch
Toilet articles as motifs, 64,72,
    92,
Train, 73
Tree, 73; see tree-of-life
Tree-of-life motif, 6, 20, 64,70,
    80-2, 109, 134
Triangle, 73, 106, 109

U

Umbrella, 73

V

Vines, 64, 82
Vishnu, 38, 89
Vedantatirtha, Girish
    Chandra, 16

W

Wajeda Begum, 75

Wall-hanging, 6, 63
Water, 70, 83,84,95
Wave, 70, 79,96,111
Weave running stitch, 50, 94,
    106-7,143
West Bengal, kantha revival
    in, 26,155-7,
Wheel, 79,127,134, 137

Y

Yarn, 24,26,35,126
Yin and yang, 70, 82